Trick School for Dogs

Manuela Zaitz

CADMOS

Copyright of original edition © 2007 by Cadmos Verlag GmbH, Im Dorfe 11, 22956 Brunsbek, Germany
Copyright of this edition © 2008 by Cadmos Books, Great Britain
Translation: Andrea Höfling
Design: Ravenstein + Partner, Verden
Photos: Andreas Maurer and Thomas Stens
Proof reading: Dr. Gabriele Lehari and Christopher Long
Printed by: agensketterl Druckerei, Mauerbach

British Library Cataloguing in Publication Data
A catalogue record of this book is available from the British Library.

Printed in Austria

ISBN 978-3-86127-960-0

Contents

Contents

Introduction

This book is suitable for both beginners and advanced tricksters. The easier tricks are explained in great detail, starting with the handshake, and working towards more difficult tricks such as balancing objects on the behind. Those of you who are already gripped by 'trick fever' will find some new ideas in this book. Some of the tricks require accessories, most of which can be found in any household, or can be rearranged with a little ingenuity.

Many tricks, such as switching on the light, originate from routines designed for the training of support and assistance dogs for the disabled. Your dog too could become a service dog, a little helper with your household chores.

In recent years, human interaction with dogs has undergone a positive change: No longer having to function solely as a working dog, your dog can now be a partner, friend and companion. A very desirable development indeed!

Basic Requirements

Initially, the basic requirements for learning tricks are time, dedication and patience. It should be easy to motivate your dog with the help of some tasty treats. Every one of us surely remembers our school days: the best conditions for learning are a relaxed environment without any stress or pressure. Turn off the television, take your time preparing the trick you want to practise, pick up the treats and then call your dog. Please don't practise at times when you're in a bad mood, irritable or impatient for whatever reason. Your dog will sense your mood, he will start feeling insecure, and the atmosphere will be tense and unpleasant for him.

There will always be situations where you can't seem to be able to make any progress with a particular trick. Don't keep trying with grim determination and clenched teeth, and above all never blame the dog. Take a break, take your dog for a nice walk, do something enjoyable and pleasant. Forget about this trick for a few days, and practise something else, before trying again.

It is helpful to have a video camera running during training sessions. Even if it does feel a bit funny at first, it helps you notice any mistakes, which you can then avoid the next time round.

As for all the jumps described in this book, you should first make sure that both dog and owner are healthy and physically capable of carrying them out. They should always be done on a soft surface – lawn or sand are very suitable. If your dog generally has trouble jumping, if he lands on his front or hind legs at an angle that is too steep, if he has a physical impairment or isn't fully grown yet, you should avoid all tricks involving jumps. Always remember that your dog's safety has to come first, and that he won't take any precautions himself. That is your responsibility.

The video is only meant for self-checking. (Photo: T. Stens)

Conditioned reinforcement

Dogs do things because they are worthwhile. A behaviour is only worthwhile, if it is reinforced. A behaviour that is worthwhile will therefore be repeated frequently. For instance praise, food or being played with are all great incentives for a dog. All these are unconditioned (primary) reinforcements. 'Unconditioned' because you don't have to teach the dog that these things are brilliant; he knows that they are worthwhile for him.

If the dog shows a desirable behaviour, you could reward him with a treat straight away. For this to work, the dog has to be very close to you at the time. The reinforcement of a behaviour displayed some distance away from you would thus be impossible. Of course you can still praise your dog by using your voice. Unfortunately, experience shows that during an average day, most dogs get so many 'text messages', they hardly pay any attention to us talking to them any more.

In this scenario, conditioned reinforcements come in very handy. Following a certain signal (a click, a tongue click or a signal word), you immediately give the dog a treat. The dog learns that the signal equals the promise of a treat. To achieve this, you need to repeat this routine again and again; every time the dog hears a signal such as a click, a tongue click or a signal chosen by you, he is rewarded with a treat. You should condition your dog to react to only one specific signal at first, otherwise things will get too confusing for him.

Clicker

The clicker really is a most useful accessory for dog training. The method of affirming an animal's action with a sound signal has become well-known through dolphin training. It quickly turned out that this way of training could achieve staggering results with other animals too.

It is important that the dog has learned the meaning of the 'click' beforehand, that he actually knows that 'click' means: 'Well done, you'll get a treat now.'

This way, you can individually encourage and shape a particular behaviour in an animal. If your dog usually has a good stretch after getting up, you can affirm the moment of the stretching and reward the dog on the spot. As most dogs will repeat worthwhile behaviour very soon – the best example is begging at the table – this way you can very easily teach your dog to take a bow.

The best thing about using a clicker is that there are no penalties. Wrong, or rather undesired behaviour is ignored, and only desired behaviour is affirmed. This encourages dogs to experiment, because they can work and try out new things without fear of reprimand.

But don't worry, if you haven't worked with a clicker yet, all tricks can be taught without a clicker as well. Having said that, I bet that once you have tried the clicker, you will not want to do without any more. It's not just that all of a sudden teaching new things becomes much easier, but it also improves the communication between dog and owner. It is marvellous to see how clicker-trained dogs offer actions, and then glance at their owner as if to say: 'Shall I do it like this? Is this what you wanted to see?'

Tongue click

If your dog often does something nicely, which you would like him to do on command as well, then you should think about conditioning your dog to react to the tongue click. Clicking with your tongue is easy. The advantage over a clicker is that you always have your tongue with you, and you will be able to affirm your dog's displayed behaviour at all times and in any situation. The conditioning is done the same way as with a 'normal' clicker. Another advantage is that you have both hands free.

You can also decide on a combination of both: to use the clicker for normal practice sessions, and the tongue click for spontaneous actions outdoors. A dog who has been conditioned to react to both will not be confused at all.

Words of praise

An enthusiastic 'Yes!' can also become a conditioned affirmation, which will show the dog the exact action for which he is being praised. To achieve this you must always try and use the same tone of voice, and of course the same term of praise. Don't say 'Great!' on one occasion, 'Fantastic!' the next, and 'Super!' the third time. Of course your dog may be able to sense your enthusiasm from the tone of your voice alone, but you'll make it that much harder for him to learn. Decide on one single word, a short one would be best, and stick to it. Condition your dog to react to this word and only use this particular word, when you want to praise him during practice for doing things the right way.

One step at a time

Taking a cursory glance at this book, you may quickly get an idea of what you would like to teach your dog first. Please pick only one exercise a time, take your time reading about the trick, and work out which basic commands you will need. If your dog hasn't mastered these yet, start with the basic commands or choose a different trick. If you require accessories, such as treats, clicker, target stick, have everything laid out ready for use, before you get the dog to join in.

Most of the tricks in this book are subdivided into small steps. Even if it is tempting to do more, please take only one step at a time. Some tricks are very complex. In order to be reliable and repeatable, the basic elements have to be in place first. It is very important to make sure the individual tricks are developed slowly and on a solid foundation. Please don't practise more than one trick at a time, as doing so would confuse not just the dog, but often the owner as well.

Be patient with your dog and don't give up. Should you fail to get to grips with a particu-

Don't expect too much of your dog at once. (Photo: T. Stens)

lar trick altogether, give it a few weeks' break, and practise something else in the meantime.

Sometimes a trick will work surprisingly well when you return to it after a pause. And if it still doesn't work, then this may just not be your dog's sort of trick. Not every dog has to be able to do everything, and each dog has his strong points and his weak points. The art is to recognise these, and this will enable you to work successfully with your dog.

Basic Commands

By basic commands, I don't mean 'Sit', 'Stay', 'Heel', or similar terms. These are certainly very important commands, which your dog has probably mastered already, but in this case I mean commands that will be needed for your dog to carry out the tricks described in this book. I am talking about recurring commands, which you can use for a huge variety of tricks and everyday things alike.

Take

The command 'Take' is supposed to prompt the dog to take in his mouth an object chosen by you. With many dogs, this is a simple matter: they have a favourite object such as a ball or a soft toy. Put the toy next to the dog and encourage him with a 'Take' to take it in his mouth. If he does so, give him instant affirmation with a click, a treat or a praise word.

Once this works well with a toy or a ball, start using everyday objects such as handkerchiefs, socks, empty cigarette packets etc.

Once this works without any problems, try your hand at more difficult things, such as bank notes, keys or similar things. Many dogs are reluctant to take metal objects in their mouths, for example keys. Make it easier for your dog by attaching a lanyard keychain to your keys, or a key fob that is easy to take hold of.

If your dog doesn't want to take the object up in his mouth, you will have to be creative. Make the object exciting, make sure it smells nice. Play with the object, but without taking any notice of your dog. Do this with such exuberance that your dog is bound to become really keen to play with it too.

Don't use any objects which you are very attached to. If you want your dog to take a telephone in his mouth, don't use your newest mobile for practice, but use a very old or defective phone. A flea market can be a treasure trove for objects to practise with.

Luke has learnt to take various objects in his mouth on the command 'Take'. (Photos: A. Maurer)

Touch

When asked to 'Touch', the dog is supposed to touch objects with his paw. There are various methods for teaching this to a dog. One is with the use of a target stick. The target stick is something you may remember from geography lessons at school: a telescopic indicator stick whose length can be adjusted like an old-fashioned car aerial. For training with a clicker there are special target sticks available, which have a slightly enlarged rounded tip. Using a fly swatter works just as well. Show your target stick to the dog, and let him examine and sniff it. If the dog uses his paws for this, affirm this behaviour.

This dog is very interested in the target stick. Here, you can see clearly how he lifts his paw in order to examine the stick more closely.

If affirmed correctly, the dog learns very quickly, what his owner is after. (Photos: A. Maurer)

At first, affirm every use of a paw, and then begin only to affirm those actions which involve the dog hitting the tip of the target stick. Introduce the command 'Touch!' for this. With the target stick you can lead your dog to the objects you want him to touch, and then prompt him with a 'Touch!' to put his paw exactly on the desired spot. It should then prove quite easy to gradually wean the dog off the target stick during the individual exercises.

Instead of the target stick, another option would be to use a sticky dot. This works best, when you attach a sticky dot to your hand first, and then have the dog put his paw on it. You gradually move the sticky dot, for example onto a finger or onto your arm. The next step could be to stick the dot on the floor. Once the dog has understood 'Touch!', you can attempt more difficult tasks, such as switching on the light. For this you simply stick the dot on the light switch. As the dog has already learnt that he must put his paw onto the dot, switching on the light is only a small step. Following the same principle, you can stick the dot on a drawer in order to teach the dog to close it.

Nudge

On the command 'Nudge!', the dog will touch objects with his nose. The simplest way to develop this is by holding your hand in front of the dog's nose, and to give affirmation as soon as he touches your hand with his nose. You can also shape the 'Nudge' command with a target stick or a sticky dot, in the same way as 'Touch'.

If the dog approaches the hand or the target, but doesn't nudge it, you can carefully push the hand or the target against the dog's nose, and follow this by instant praise, as if the dog had managed it all by himself. Every time the dog's

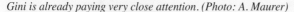

Gini is already paying very close attention. (Photo: A. Maurer)

nose touches the target or your hand, you say 'Nudge!' Repeat this several times, until the dog has understood that every nose-target contact results in a treat. Now hold the target in front of his nose once more. Hold it quite close to the dog's nose, in order to make it as easy for him as possible. If you see a small movement in the direction of the target stick, give the command 'Nudge!' When he does the nudge for the first time without any help, reward him instantly with a jackpot.

Pull

This command is best taught to your dog during a 'tug of war' game, during which you cheer the dog on by using the command 'Pull!' Take an old towel and let him pull it from your fingers. If the dog isn't keen to join in at first, wave the towel around with fast and jerky movements, while making wild squealing noises. If he takes it into his mouth, pull on it for only a split second, and then let the dog win

Nudge! (Photo: A. Maurer)

The 'pull' command can also be used to make the dog pull a toy car behind him. (Photo: A. Maurer)

and play with his prey. This game is self-rewarding, therefore there is hardly any need for treats. Repeat this game again and again, in between other activities. In order to see whether the dog has understood the command, and has made the right associations, take the towel lightly in your hand and, while omitting the previous 'tug of war' game, just ask the dog to pull the towel by using the command 'Pull!' If he pulls it from your hand, reward him with a jackpot.

Make sure, however, that the pulling action doesn't get out of control. At a later stage, when the dog is asked to remove your socks, it would not be particularly pleasant if he were to end up shaking your leg vigorously in the process.

Fetch

This is an extension of the 'Take!' command. The dog is supposed to bring you an object chosen at random on command. If your dog is not yet able to 'Fetch', begin with a step-by-step approach. Take one of your dog's toys and place it directly in front of your feet. Encourage your dog to take the toy using the command 'Fetch!' Exchange the toy he has just picked up with an especially tasty treat. Very important: return the toy to your dog afterwards. Giving up a desired object is not particularly easy for a dog. Your aim, however, is that your dog should be eager to bring you anything you ask for, therefore you have to make it worthwhile for him. A tasty treat or a nice game is a suitable reinforcement. If your dog is standing in front of you with an object

This nine-month-old border collie has already learnt to eagerly fetch various objects. (Photo: A. Maurer)

in his mouth, and you offer him a tasty treat in exchange, he will drop the object. Take the toy and give him the treat. Once this works well, put the toy on the floor a few centimetres away.

Increase the distance further and further, but make sure you do things really slowly, step by step, in order to develop the command with solid foundations.

Put it in my hand

The dog places an object in your hand. For this trick, your dog already needs to be able to pick up objects in his mouth, and to bring them to you. If he is unable to do this yet, start with the previous exercise, and once your dog has mastered the 'Fetch!' command, continue from this point onwards.

The dog is standing in front of you with the object in his mouth. Place your hand directly below your dog's jaw and hold a treat in front of his nose with the other hand. The moment he opens his mouth to take the treat, you say 'Give it to me!', or a different command of your choice. Whatever command you choose, it should be clearly distinguishable from the 'Let go!' command. Once he has eaten the treat, encourage him to pick up the object once more, and repeat the action of 'Put it in my hand' several times. If your dog doesn't want to let go of the object, try the same routine using a less attractive object, a folded pair of socks, perhaps, or something similar.

Once the 'Put it into my hand' routine is working well, increase the difficulty by placing your hand not directly under his jaw, but a few centimetres to one side. If your dog has understood the command, he will place the object in your hand. Reward him instantly with a jackpot. If the object falls to the ground, because your dog hasn't yet made the right associations with the command, go back one step and practise several more times with your hand under his jaw, before making any fresh attempts. The aim is to have the dog place objects in your hand, no matter how high you hold it. Of course you'll have to take into account the physical limitations of your dog.

Up

This is a nice simple command. At the command, the dog is supposed to jump on a chair, a table or a sofa. Make sure that the objects you want your dog to jump onto are safe and the right height for his size. They should also be sturdy, and not liable to slide or topple over. Lure the dog towards you with a treat.

Dando approaches with the purse…

…and places it carefully in his owner's hand.
(Photos: A. Maurer)

This usually works really well, when practising a jump on the sofa. The moment the dog is about to jump, you give the chosen command, for example 'Up!'

Praise your dog, immediately when he has landed on the object of your choice.

Don't do this exercise too many times in a row, because excessive jumping can put too much strain on your dog's muscles, joints and tendons.

Down

The dog is supposed to jump off an object on command. If, up to now, you used to push your dog off the sofa using the command 'Down!', he will not associate this command with anything particularly positive. It would be better to lure your dog to jump off a particular object with the help of a treat, and to give the 'Down!' command the moment he is about to jump.

When you have taken your dog on a drive, you can also choose the command you use to get him to jump out of the car.

Stop

The dog is supposed to stand still on the spot at the command 'Stop!' This can be useful when the dog is supposed to carry out a trick

Matjes is being encouraged with a treat to jump on the box.

A hand signal is enough to make Matjes jump off the box. (Photos: A. Maurer)

This Border Collie stops in its tracks as soon as the hand is stretched out. (Photo: A. Maurer)

in a particular part of the room, but it is also an important command for everyday life, which your dog should definitely be able to obey.

First of all, put your dog on a leash. Lead him around for a while, making sure that you don't tug or pull on the leash. Walk at a slow pace and make sure that your dog's head is about knee level. Hold the leash with the hand that is on the same side your dog is walking on.

Continuing the slow movement, turn your upper body towards your dog, hold out your hand, say 'Stop!' and stop walking. Repeat this frequently, for example every time you encounter a road crossing during your walks,

but also, whilst at home. Make sure you don't subconsciously tighten the leash when you give the command 'Stop!', because the aim of this exercise is for your dog to be able to carry out the command when he is not on the leash, and at a greater distance.

The outstretched hand stops the dog, and is a visual signal at the same time. Later, it will be sufficient to just stretch out the hand in order to stop the dog. For this, you increase the level of difficulty step by step. Practise it while walking at heel without a leash. Once this works well, increase the difficulty and stand two paces away from your dog. If he comes towards you, you say 'Stop!', and

It's the same at a distance: The outstretched hand means 'Stop!' (Photo: A. Maurer)

stretch your hand out towards him. If he stops, he has earned a jackpot! Praise him enthusiastically, and practise at a distance of three paces the next time round. Slowly increase the level of difficulty, and practise in different locations, in order for your dog to learn that this command applies anywhere.

Should the dog not stop at your command, go back to the point where it worked well. Take smaller steps to continue. This may take a bit more time, but it is important to build the foundations for the commands very thoroughly and in a positive way.

Important Things for the Trick School

Visual signals and voice commands

I have given names to many tricks and suggested a suitable command for them. Of course you can be creative and use your own individual commands. When you introduce a command, make sure you say the command at the moment when you're quite certain that the dog is just about to carry out the desired action. At the beginning this applies even when the desired action is only happening with your help or with the help of a treat.

If you intend to introduce a visual signal with a trick, do start practising it right from the start. Dogs communicate with each other via body language, and always interpret our body posture. The introduction of visual signals is therefore very helpful for the dog.

For Benda the upward-pointing index finger is the visual signal for the command 'Sit!' When practised sufficiently, this will work in unusual environments as well. (Photo: T. Stens)

Reward, affirmation and appropriate treats

In the description of every trick, the terms affirmation and reward are used. There is no such thing as an ideal reward, this depends very much on the individual dog. There are dogs who will do a lot of work for their dog biscuits and who will co-operate enthusiastically, but this is not necessarily always the case. Try to give a stronger incentive by choosing a more attractive affirmation. Try using ready-made treats or strong-smelling cheese, chicken or turkey sausages, dried fish or small dried strips of lung. Boil up some chicken meat or chicken hearts and find out what makes your dog work best. For some tricks, it is advisable to use slightly less attractive treats, because otherwise the apparent level of difficulty is unnecessarily increased. This issue will be dealt with separately later in the description. Don't forget to reduce your dog's daily food ration according to the amount of treats you give him as a reward, otherwise you will soon have an overweight dog on your hands. For some dogs, a game with their favourite ball can also represent a treat. Many dogs, however, will prefer a tasty treat, and for working on most tricks, this is certainly the best choice.

Whichever kind of affirmation you decide on, always remember that for a reward or affirmation to work, you have a limited hold of a maximum of only two seconds. Only during this brief interval does the dog have the ability to make an association between praise and action. The greater the proximity between the praise or affirmation, and the desired action, the better.

Treats or games – there are many possibilities for praising or affirming your dog. (Photo: A. Maurer)

Jackpot

You would like your dog to carry out tricks without treats as well? Ask yourself, whether you would be happy to work for a slap on the back from your boss, or if you wouldn't rather get paid a proper salary instead.

The motivation has to fit the bill; this is not so different for a dog than it is for us humans. It's only the things that motivate us that are different. Certainly, once a trick or a command has been well-established, you don't have to affirm your dog every time, but you should still reward him every now and then randomly, and for the dog unpredictably. This will ensure continued motivation and eagerness to work.

A jackpot is the ultimate reward. It consists of a particularly tasty treat which you give to your dog instead of the usual treat, after he has made an absolutely fantastic effort. Traditionally, however, a jackpot means that the dog gets a whole load of treats, as opposed to just one. Use this jackpot for those moments when it becomes obvious that the dog has just taken a large leap forward. Reward him as soon as possible, and with adequate enthusiasm. The dog should be made to realise how pleased you are with his excellent achievement. Jackpots will keep a dog's motivation at a really high level, and increase his willingness to perform.

Training duration

Reading through the descriptions of the individual tricks, you may perhaps think: 'Great, let's do this straight away!' It is good to have an enthusiastic attitude, and if you approach these things with a sense of fun, your dog will take

Make sure you have regular intervals, and break up the practice session into small, manageable units. (Photo: A. Maurer)

his cue from you. Remember, however, that a dog is unable to keep working on a trick continually for a whole half-hour. The receptive capacity of an individual dog depends on several factors: age, environment, temperature, time of day, mood, mode of learning.

Try to stick to a limit of five minutes' practice at a time; if you have a very motivated dog, you may extend this to ten minutes, but this should be an exception. It would be better to practise on several different occasions each day. Some exercises can easily be integrated into your everyday routines or into your walks. Several smaller units will provide a good success rate, the dog has the opportunity to spend quality time with you several times a day, and will be 'reminded' of the things he has learnt over and over again. Don't expect too much, either of yourself or of your dog. Some tricks require a lot of practice, and certainly cannot be mastered in a single day. Don't be discouraged by this. Practise in many steps, and be pleased about every small, partial success too.

Signal control

If a trick or a behaviour is governed by signal control, and the dog displays this behaviour every time you give the command, then you must ignore the behaviour in the event that the dog displays it without the command being given. Don't be tempted to reward it, even if it is carried out to perfection. Otherwise, some dogs have a tendency to reel off their repertory time and time again, in the hope of reaping a reward. As a result, the dog will become inattentive and unreceptive. Ignore him, and once he has calmed down, give him a different command, for which you can then reward him.

Generalising

If a trick or a command is always practised in the same place, for example in the living room, and the dog has mastered the command to perfection, this does not mean that he will remember this command when it is given outside on the lawn. Therefore it is best to rotate the place of practice frequently. You could sometimes practise in the living room, sometimes in the bedroom, or in the garden, or in town, or in the car park. You should also vary your body posture. Experiment by giving your dog a simple command, while lying down outside on the lawn. If your dog obeys the vocal command straight away, he has generalised the command. No matter where you are, or how you behave, he still knows what the command means.

At first, however, most dogs will be so confused that they won't be able to perform the desired action. This is no cause for worry, but do try to practise these things nevertheless. It will firm up the commands, and will make them more reliable no matter what the circumstances are.

Commands, and how to make an even bigger impression

There are several possibilities to combine the different tricks with voice- or visual signals. If you want to use these tricks for little shows, performances or castings, it would make sense to skilfully work the commands into your speech.

For example, if you want to impress your guests at home by having your dog turn the light on, then use the command 'Light!' As soon as your dog has mastered the exercise, work the signal word into a sentence. Say, for example: 'It's rather dark here, I need more light.' After sufficient practice, the dog will filter out the signal word and press the light switch – and your guests will be suitably impressed.

Or choose the command 'Socks!', for taking off your socks. This can also be worked into a sentence really well: 'I'm so tired, can you please take off my socks?' Bear in mind, however, that before you can begin to work a voice signal into a sentence, the dog must be able to carry out the action without fail prompted by the signal word on its own.

Over-emphasise the signal word at the beginning, until you can use a normal tone of voice.

Bear in mind that while he is peacefully asleep, your dog will not hear these sentences. In order to induce receptiveness, you can introduce a 'Watch out, here comes a command!' word. This will attract the dog's attention, so the dog knows that a command is imminent. If you want to keep this 'advance warning' inconspicuous to an unsuspecting spectator, you could always choose a sigh with an 'Oh dear', for this purpose. In order to firm this up, you will, however, need to carry out a great many repetitions in connection with the vocal signals. Begin to sigh with an 'Oh dear' and give your dog a treat afterwards. Repeat this several times a day. As soon as your dog approaches you attentively upon hearing these words, you begin to demand a trick before rewarding him. In order to prevent the 'advanced warning' from wearing off, you should reinforce it from time to time at irregular intervals.

Working at a distance

Tricks are wonderful things, but they make an even bigger impression when they are performed at a distance. Of course, a beautifully exercised 'Shame in you!' will look just as impressive when it is carried out at your feet. Nevertheless, you should work at achieving a good result, even when there is a five-metre distance between you and your dog. This, however, has to be achieved centimetre by centimetre. First, walk away half a pace before giving the chosen command. Once this works, you can increase the distance by taking these steps. Don't forget to reward your dog every time he performs a trick well. If you realise that your dog experiences problems from a certain distance onward, stand at least one pace closer to him, and keep this up for about five or six exercise units. Afterwards carefully 'feel' your way towards taking half a pace backwards again, and from there increase the distance, little by little. The beauty of working at a distance is that the dog doesn't mind which command he is given; a 'Sit!' or 'Down!' is just as possible from further away, once the dog is used to working at a distance.

Setting up chains of actions

Some tricks, like for example 'stealing money', are developed using a complex chain of actions. In order to make it as easy as possible for the dog, begin with the last part of the trick. Once the dog has mastered this part, add the penultimate part, practise this, and attach it to the final part, so that eventually you have linked up several segments of the complete trick. This has the advantage that the dog already knows the part of the trick that follows the part which he has to learn from scratch. Thus he knows that he will always at least have one success and that he will be able to earn a reward for himself. Slowly work your way through the trick from back to front, until you have created a complete chain of action.

In order to avoid mistakes regarding the structure of the trick, it makes sense to write down the trick with all its details, then break it up into its separate components, and then put them into the right order for training. Don't practise too much at once, instead put the building blocks together slowly, in order to achieve a good stable foundation.

'No!'

With some dogs it might be useful to introduce a sort of 'What a pity, no reward' command, because in certain situations you may have to stop the dog in mid-action during training. To use 'No!' as your usual command to effect an interruption would be counterproductive. Because of its negative connotations, many dogs stop volunteering actions as a result. It would be more advisable to use a new signal which says: 'What you're doing now will not lead to a reward.'

In order to set this up, you sit down in front of the dog, holding treats in both hands and giving them to the dog with one hand in short intervals. When the dog starts enjoying this beautiful situation, you close the hand which is dispensing the treats, and say 'Naah, in a calm and neutral tone of voice. Alternatively you could say 'Too bad!', or something similar as a signal word. If the dog turns to the other hand, he will get a treat from that hand. In order to make it easier for him at the beginning, you could gently move the other hand around a bit, in order to draw his attention to the alternative. This way he will learn that 'Too bad - no reward' does not have to lead to complete frus-

tration, but that he has a real chance to earn a reward by changing his behaviour.

Training diary

Most dog owners aren't sure how much their dog actually understands. If you write down all the commands, it often turns out that there are surprisingly many. Make a note of all the commands, together with the relevant voice/sound and visual signals, and keep updating this list. Write down what you always wanted to teach your dog, so you don't run out of ideas for the next training unit. When practising chains of actions, write down how they are broken up into various individual steps or segments.

If your dog has a tendency to be easily distracted and lose concentration, note down the external circumstances, such as training location, weather, your dog's mood and your own, telephone calls and other interruptions, the kind of treat used and the progress you have made on every training day. When you have observed this for a few weeks, you will develop a better understanding of how your dog works, and you will be able to filter out the optimum learning conditions for him. If you have more than one dog, or if you are working with several dogs, you will quickly be able to identify the strengths and weaknesses of each individual dog and deal with them accordingly.

Tricks

Jumping over an arm or a leg

The jump over an arm or a leg is often seen as part of Dog Dance or during Dog Frisbee free-style routines . You can use this jump in many variations and adapt it to the different require-ments of the dog and his owner. The height of the jump depends on the dog's size. The dog has to be healthy and fully-grown. If you or your dog suffer from a physical impairment of any kind, you should choose a different trick.

In order to get the dog used to this unusual situation, make sure you start at a very low height.

Squat down in a sort of 'Cossack' position, and stretch one leg out. Lure your dog into jumping over your leg, with a treat or a toy. The moment the dog is about to jump, you give the command 'Jump!' Sometimes it can be helpful to have a second person to assist, if the dog is very excited and fidgety. The assistant can briefly hold the dog, until you have safely squatted down and are holding the treat on the correct side of your leg. Only then is the dog sent on his mission. If the dog walks around the leg instead of jumping over it, you can do this exercise in a tight spot, such as a doorframe, where there is insufficient space to walk around. As ever, make sure that you're doing this on a non-slip surface.

Once the dog jumps confidently and without any problems, you can vary the height. Always bear in mind your dog's physical capabilities and limitations.

Laika is very slowly and carefully led across the outstretched leg.

'Play dead'

The dog lies motionless on the floor. This exercise is not easy for agile dogs who like to move around a lot. With the help of a treat, you can lure the dog from the 'down' position into lying on his side. To do this, you move a treat in front of the dog's nose towards his shoulder blade in a semi-circle. In order to be able to follow the treat with his nose and eyes, the dog is forced to drop on his side. Affirm the dog with a treat, even when only his body is lying down, while his head is still eagerly looking around. You can slowly bring his head a little closer to the floor

After a little practice, most dogs manage a jump over a slightly raised leg without any problem. (Photos: A. Maurer)

With a treat, the Border Collie Emma is manoeuvred into the correct position. (Photo: A. Maurer)

by dispensing further treats. Don't push the dog onto the ground, as he may misunderstand this. Also you want to work out this trick together with your dog, as opposed to simply pushing him into the correct position.

The instant your dog allows his head to sink sideways as well, you give the command 'Play dead!' and reward him with a treat. But what can you do, if the dog gets up again every time, instead of dropping on his side, as you try luring him with a treat into a lying-down on his side position? There can be several reasons for this. Some dogs, for instance, don't like lying on wet surfaces such as dewy grass. Some dogs actually find floor tiles too hard to lie on. In such a case, a change of surface may be helpful. Also the treat may simply be too good, and perhaps using a drier, slightly less

'Play dead' at a distance. (Photo: A. Maurer)

tasty treat might help. Some dogs find it unsettling when a hand moves in the direction of their neck, because they may have had bad experiences with humans in the past. If nothing else seems to work, think of situations in which your dog would lie on his side voluntarily, and affirm him when he does so. This may take longer, but may possibly save you and your dog a lot of stress.

Barking

The dog begins to bark at you on command. There are dogs that have a tendency to bark, while others can barely be persuaded to utter a quiet 'woof'. For both types of dog the development of the exercise is the same, but the intensity varies greatly.

If your dog barks a lot across the fence at the neighbour's dog, then this is not a situation in which you'd want to affirm your dog's beha-

Australian shepherd Dando would dearly like to get hold of the ball.

Thus provoked, he begins to bark.

After a short time the dog begins to bark when prompted by a hand signal. (Photos: A. Maurer)

viour. The learning success achieved by this exercise would be zero. Instead, take one of your dog's favourite toys and play with it exuberantly, but without letting your dog join in. Provoke him with it, but under no circumstances allow him to get hold of it.

Most dogs will begin to bark soon enough out of frustration. Affirm your dog straight away, and preferably with the toy, because at this particular moment this is what he'd really, really like.

Repeat this exercise several times. Once you are sure that the dog will display the bark again, add the command 'Speak!'

However, in order to avoid teaching your dog to become a yapper who will bark every time he wants something from you, you will have to stop any undesirable barking at the same time as you are introducing the command. The best way of doing this is by turning and walking away. If the dog then goes quiet, praise and reward him. It would be useful to introduce a command such as 'Quiet!' or 'Shush!', as well.

Snoopy hesitantly touches the hand with his paw.

Shake a paw

This must be the most classical of all dog tricks, and the one that most dogs will be able to perform. The dog places his paw in your hand on command.

Take a treat in your hand and close your fingers to make a fist while the dog is watching. Hold out your closed fist towards the dog at chest height. Initially, the dog will try to sniff the treat, and then he'll try to get to it. If the dog uses his paw to scratch at the hand, affirm him instantly.

You can now let him have the treat you're holding in your closed hand, or – and this is even better – give him a new treat with the other hand. Some dogs seem to believe otherwise, that the point of the exercise is to dig the treat out of the hand, and they don't know what they are supposed to do about a hand, that

Learning quickly! (Photos: T. Stens)

High five

obviously contains no treat. You can avoid this by giving the reward with the other hand. When you see the dog lift his paw in order to touch your hand, give the command 'paw' or a different command of your choice for this exercise.

What should you do if your dog shows no reaction? There are some dogs that will just sit in front of the closed hand and stare. Open your hand again to show him the treat, sniff it yourself in an interested manner, and close your hand again. Change your position and move a few metres back, in order to add a bit of movement to the situation. If this still doesn't lead to success, you can take the dog's paw in your hand, and then reward him. But because this solution doesn't require him to use his brainpower, it is possible that you may need to repeat the latter exercise much more often in order for the command to sink in permanently.

As a variation, you can alternate between shaking paws with the right paw or with the left. Prompted by the command, the dog is supposed to offer the paw you have asked for. You should give some thought to which command you want to use for each paw respectively. If you choose 'Right!' and 'Left!', it will be more difficult to insert the command into your speech. If on top of that, the dog's owner is having difficulties telling their right from their left (not unheard of), the dog will get unnecessarily confused. 'Hello!' for one paw and 'Bye-bye!' for the other would also make good commands.

You often see the 'high five' used by athletes – the slapping together of hands with arms outstretched above the head. It sounds complicated, but is really a relatively easy to learn variation of the paw-shake. Before attempting this, your dog needs to be able to do the paw-shake. Start changing your hand position. If before you held out your hand towards your dog, intending a handshake, now your fingertips should point upwards and the palms of your hands towards your dog. Hold your hand just above the height of your dog's chest. Initially, the dog will perhaps just brush against your hand with his paw. This would be quite good already, and you should reward it adequately. If your dog manages to push his paw against your hand – even if only for the shortest of moments – you should praise him with enthusiasm and reward him with a jackpot. As soon as the dog lifts a paw in order the put it against your hand, give the command 'High five!'

Paws stretched up high and hands outstretched – this is what it should look like. (Photo: A. Maurer)

Twist and fox

The dog is chasing his tail. This exercise is easy to learn and can be worked out with the help of the target stick or simply with a treat. Dog and owner are facing each other. Show the treat to your dog, and slowly, so the dog can follow it easily, describe a wide semi-circle from his nose in the direction of his tail. If your dog follows the movement, add the vocal command 'Twist!'

In order to lure your dog into a turning movement, you have no choice but to lean over your dog. Some dogs will find this unpleasant, as it can appear quite menacing. Observe your dog closely. Should your dog display signs of uneasiness, use a target stick instead, if he has already learnt to follow one. You will find the instructions for the target stick earlier on in this book. Once you have managed a complete circle affirm the dog and repeat the exercise.

The dog can turn in either a clockwise or an anti-clockwise direction. Most dogs find one direction easier than the other. To begin with, only practise one direction, and once that works really well, attempt the circle in the other direction. Choose two different commands for turning in the two different directions, for example 'Twist!' and 'Fox!' In order to make the distinction easier for the dog to understand by the use of visual signals, it would make sense to have the dog follow the treat in your right hand for the clockwise turn, and in your left hand for the anti-clockwise turn. Later you can use just a visual signal for the turn. Depending on whether you give the signal with your right hand or your left hand, you determine the direction.

It can be done standing up too. (Photo: A. Maurer)

Small dogs tend to sit high on their hind legs while doing this. This looks nice and is a great variation which can also be practised with larger dogs, if they have already mastered the high five while sitting down. You just have to hold your hand a bit higher, so that the dog has to raise his front paws in order to reach your hand.

Using the right hand, the dog is guided into doing the clockwise 'Twist'.

For the 'Fox', it's best to move the treat around with your other hand. (Photos: A. Maurer)

Roll-over

The dog does a 360-degree roll-over. Please bear in mind that with larger breeds there is always a risk of gastric torsion. Please don't do this trick if there is an inherent tendency in your dog's breed for this to happen. No dogs should be fed for about three hours before this exercise. Have your dog lie down and make sure he is lying in a relaxed, slightly sideways position, with both his hind legs pointing to one side. Take a treat and guide it in a semi-circle from the dog's nose towards his shoulder blade in the direction of the same side to which his legs are pointing. If the dog follows the treat by turning his head, he has to drop on his side, in order not to lose sight of it. Some dogs jump up every time at this point, so that they never complete the roll-over. If this happens, you should affirm your dog when he is on his side. Guide the treat slowly further across his body, so that he can follow it with his eyes and his head. As soon as he has turned his body around so far that his legs point in the other direction, affirm him.

During the development of this trick you give the command 'Roll over!' every time the dog actually does roll over his back. Gradually reduce the use of treats as a guiding aid, and only reward the dog when he has done a complete roll-over.

Waving

A nice variation of the 'handshake' is the wave with a paw. The structure is very similar to the 'handshake'. Hold out your hand towards your dog. If he tries to put his paw in your hand, withdraw your hand quickly and affirm your dog for hitting the air. Give the command 'Wave!'

Laika keeps an eye on the treat and rolls around her own axis. (Photos: A. Maurer)

A wave from you as a visual signal for your dog is a lovely idea. (Photo: A. Maurer)

Shame on you!

The dog puts one paw over his nose or wipes across his nose with his paw.

This is a cute trick which is always appreciated by any audience. You can use a variety of accessories for this: a Post-it note, a piece of sticky tape that has been prepared in advance so it doesn't stick too well, or a cotton thread.

Have the dog sit down and put a cotton thread on his nose. Most dogs will instantly a Post-it instead of the thread. A Post-it is ideal, because it sticks, but doesn't pull the dog's hair when he wipes it off. If you are using a piece of sticky tape, press it against a towel several times beforehand to reduce its stickiness. Make sure that your dog doesn't feel any discomfort. Vary the spot until you have found the optimal point on your dog's nose.

When you have stuck on the strip of sticky tape and you are sure that your dog will now display the paw-wiping action, you can add the chosen command such as 'Shame on you!', or something similar. Practise and affirm this frequently and in quick succession. Then try it without any aids or accessories. Give your dog the command and wait and see if he performs the action. If he does not yet display it without the aid of sticky tape or cotton thread, you'll have to continue for a while longer, until he has completely understood what is expected of him.

Alsation-mix Luke attempts to wipe off the cotton thread with great accuracy.

try to get rid of the thread. If the dog uses his paw for this, affirm him straight away, and repeat the exercise. Sometimes you just have to identify the most effective spot the thread. If you put the thread too far forward, the dog may not even notice it there, and not display any action.

If your dog lowers his head and the thread just falls off on its own, it may be better to use

A Post-it is wiped off too.
(Photos: A. Maurer)

Poodle-half-breed Ronja is ready.

A successful walk-through will instantly be rewarded. (Photos: A. Maurer)

Slalom

The dog weaves through the owner's legs from left to right, while the owner moves either forwards or backwards. This exercise, often seen at Dog Dance or Frisbee events, can easily be practised while out walking. To co-ordinate treats, legs, and dog can often look easier than it is. Choose the side with which you want to begin.

Take the dog on your left side, for example. Put your right foot in front and your left foot slightly behind, so as to provide a passage for the dog. As a general rule, you should remember to always stand facing the dog with your upper body. If the dog were to stand on your right side, with this leg position you would have to twist around a lot in order to see and affirm the dog.

Take the treat in your right hand and lure the dog to walk through your legs. If he follows your hand, affirm him instantly with a treat. Take a step forward. Now your left leg is in front and the dog is positioned on your right side. Take a treat into your left hand, and lure the dog through your legs once more. Every time the dog is about to walk through your legs, give the command 'Weave!'

To begin with, this will look a little stiff and awkward, but with time the exercise will become more fluid. Once the walking through the legs is working well, reinforce this behaviour only every second or third time, and stand in a more and more upright position. For very small dogs it makes sense to use a target stick, if the dog has already learned to follow the target. This way you don't have to bend down so low.

Some dogs have a big problem with their owner leaning over them like that, and they refuse to walk through the legs. In this case you can try the target stick and turn your upper body away from the dog, in order to appear less menacing. Or you can roll a ball or a treat through your legs, so the dog follows these. In order to prevent your dog from just running around you on the outside, you should pick a strategically suitable spot, such as a doorframe, for this exercise.

Figure-of-eight

This exercise is basically just a variation of the slalom, while you stay in one place.

Stand with your legs apart and with the dog on your left side. Bend the right knee slightly, and lure the dog with a treat from the front left to the right side of your back leg, by holding the treat in your right hand between your legs and easily visible from behind. If the dog is positioned on your right side, bend the left knee slightly and guide the dog with a treat through

What seems like rather hard work at the beginning, later on appears fluid and easy without the accessories. (Photos: A. Maurer)

your legs from the front left to right side of your back leg. This bending of the knee will later serve as the visual signal for your dog to indicate the figure-of-eight through the legs. If your dog can already do the slalom through the legs, you can use the same command for the figure-of-eight at the beginning.

Play Bow

This exercise is called 'bow'. 'Taking a bow' is also a good way of putting it, and is often performed at the end of Dog Dance routines. Kneel or stand next to your dog, which should be standing up. Hold the treat in the hand which points towards the dog's head. Extend the other hand lightly under the dog's tummy. Let the dog sniff the treat and then move your hand slowly downward between the dog's front paws. If the dog follows with his nose and head, pull the hand with the treat further forward between the paws. In the past you may have taught your dog the command 'Down!' the same way. Now you use your other hand, which is held under the dog's abdomen to prevent the dog from lowering his rump onto the ground. As the dog lowers the front of his body downwards you give your chosen command, for example 'Bow!'

Some dogs may feel very uncomfortable when they feel a hand under their tummy, and may

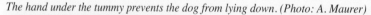

The hand under the tummy prevents the dog from lying down. (Photo: A. Maurer)

make evasive moves, or lie down flat on their tummy. In this case, try a different approach. Sit down on the floor with the dog on your left side, and with your left leg extended and the right leg bent. Lure the dog with a treat, to walk over your left leg and under your right leg. Because of the left leg lying down, the dog cannot put his rear end on the ground, and because of the right bent leg he can't raise his front. Affirm him in this position. For larger dogs the bent leg will not offer enough space to accommodate the dog. In this case, position yourself against a doorframe and hold your leg at the right height for your dog to fit in the gap underneath.

As a third option you could capture this behaviour with the clicker. Many dogs display the low front position when they have been lying down for a long time and are having a good stretch after getting up. If you frequently give him a click at this moment, chances are that the dog will offer this behaviour voluntarily.

Jumping over someone's back

If your dog has mastered the jump across a leg, you already have the basic building blocks in place. You can even use the same command for jumping across any body parts, such as arms, legs, tummy and back. Because of the different body positions required by the individual exer-

The bent leg prevents the dog from raising up his front, the extended leg prevents the dog from lowering his rear onto the ground. (Photo: A. Maurer)

cises, it is possible to do this without confusing the dog.

During the learning phase you should give the command 'Jump!' just at the point when the dog is about to jump across the respective body part. If your dog suffers any physical impairment, please don't use this trick.

At the beginning, you should only practise this trick with some assistants. (Photo: A. Maurer)

The jump across the tummy is a little easier, and there is no need for an assistant. For smaller dogs, you can start by lying on your back. The dog is positioned on your left side. Lure the dog towards you, with a toy or a treat in your right hand. If he tries to walk around you, once again lie down in a narrow spot or use some obstacles to block the way around you. Bear in mind that your dog may not jump across your whole body in one go, but use your tummy as a springboard instead. Depending on the size and weight of the dog, this could be quite painful. Whatever you do, don't punish your dog. This is a new situation for him, and without your instigation it would never have crossed his mind to jump over you in the first place.

If you have a larger dog, you can also sit down on the floor with bent legs. Put your hands behind you about as far apart as the width of your hips, and lift your bottom off the ground. Now the dog can jump sideways across you. Once you have made sure that you are in a stable position, encourage your dog to jump. You may need the help of an assistant at the beginning.

The same goes for the jump across the back. Initially, it would be best to have two people to assist you with this. Kneel on a soft surface and prop up both your arms at approximately the width of your shoulders. Make sure that your back is sufficiently protected from being scratched by your dog's claws, by wearing several T-shirts on top of each other, or a neoprene waistcoat. You should avoid slippery upper body garments which would not offer your dog any foothold. He needs to feel confident and

The help of a second person makes this exercise easier until the dog jumps confidently and securely. (Photo: A. Maurer)

You need to stand in a secure position in order to have your dog jump across your back. (Photo: T. Stens)

secure when he jumps across your back. The assistants position themselves close to your right and to your left side. One assistant lures the dog across your back with a treat, using your behind as a starting point. The treat must be positioned in such a way that the dog can only reach it after he has completed the jump. Link this with your chosen command for this exercise.

If, after a few repetitions, this exercise works well, try it without the assistant. It is possible that now, instead of jumping on your back, your dog may walk around you. If this happens, go back a step and continue practising with two assistants. Once your dog jumps confidently and without fear with just one assistant, you can make another attempt without any assistants at all, after a few more exercises.

Depending on the dog's size, you can also teach your four-legged friend to jump on your back and to stop there. This trick is developed in a similar way to the jump across the back, and once again you will need assistance. This time, the assistant holds the treat at approximately the same height as your neck, so that in order to reach the treat the dog will have to put his front paws at about the height of your shoulder blades. Choose the command 'Up!' for this, the same command used for the jump on top of an object. The gradual elimination of assistance and accessories works in the same way as described above. If your dog is not too heavy, and good at jumping, you can also have him jump on top of your back while you are standing in a bent-over position. This is another exercise that is often seen at Dog Dance or Frisbee events. If your dog is a bit on the large side, you should probably not entertain such plans.

Taking socks off

The dog carefully pulls off the owner's socks.

It would be best to use a big, firm woollen sock at the beginning, which fits rather loosely on the foot. First of all, hold the sock loosely in your hand, show it to your dog and encourage him to take hold of it. If your dog has already mastered 'Take!' and 'Pull!', you can make use of these. Just have your dog pull the loosely held sock out of your hand at first. Reward him and repeat the exercise, until you're quite sure your dog will pull the sock.

The initial interest in the sock is aroused …

…and here it's already being pulled off.
(Photos: A. Maurer)

Put the sock on the tip of your foot so it is just covering your toes. Show the sock to your dog. If the dog takes the sock and pulls it off your toes, praise him enthusiastically and make it a little bit more difficult for him each time after that. It can take quite a while until the dog will be able to pull a sock off a foot, that has been put on all the way. If you want to make an even bigger impression, you can gradually move on to thinner socks. Pulling a thin summer sock off a foot is noticeably more difficult.

Following the same principle, you can practise pulling off gloves, or pulling a shoelace open.

Home

The dog stands in front of you and facing you, then turns around and walks backwards through your legs.

Stand with your legs slightly apart while holding a treat. The dog is standing in front of you, looking at you. Show him the treat, hold it in front of his nose and move your hand in a wide semi-circle towards his rear. Move your hand slowly so that the dog can follow your hand easily. Now the dog is still standing in front of you, but facing you with his hindquarters. Use the treat to lure him backwards through your legs.

It would be an advantage if you have already practised the walking backwards exercise beforehand. As soon as the dog starts moving backwards through your legs, you give the

The dog is made to walk backwards with the help of a treat.

After a bit of practice, the dog can do the 'Home!'. (Photos: A. Maurer)

command 'Home!' At the beginning, reward even the smaller steps. Later, you should reward him only when the dog has passed through your legs completely, so he is actually standing behind you.

Later, for most dogs a mere hand signal is often sufficient, which is usually a very toned-down version of the earlier, wide circular movement with the treat.

You can combine the whole thing with the 'Polonaise' exercise, for example to perform at a Dog Dance event.

Opening a zip

The dog opens a zip. For this you can use a jacket or a bag with a zip that works smoothly without getting stuck. Attach a piece of cord to the slider itself, so the dog will be able to take hold of the zip and pull the zip open. Some jackets or bags have a zip tag already, so you can make use of that as well. Show the zip to the dog and ask him to take the zip using the command 'Take!'

Reward him instantly and repeat this exercise until the dog takes the zip tag in his mouth, voluntarily and eagerly. Then advance one step further and ask him to pull the zip, using the command 'Pull!' If the zip moves – even by just a few millimetres – praise the dog enthusiastically.

Practise this until the dog manages to open the zip completely.

Scully carefully takes the cord attached to the zip.

Once the dog has understood this exercise, he will open the zip right to the end. (Photos: A. Maurer)

Taking a jacket off

For this exercise it is important that the dog has already mastered the zip-opening routine. Pick a jacket that is perhaps a bit on the old and robust side, as the dog is going to pull the sleeve later. The zip should work smoothly and not get stuck easily, even when pulled at different angles. Attach a little piece of cord to this zip too. If you have not used this jacket for the zip-opening routine before, don't expect your dog to automatically realise that he is dealing with a zip and how to open it. Dogs are really bad at generalising, so you have to help by reminding him of his previously acquired knowledge. Put the jacket on the ground or your lap, depending on your dog's size, and practise the zip opening once more, as described previously.

When this works well, put on the jacket and kneel in front of your dog. The zip should be positioned at an easy-to-reach height for the dog. Encourage him to take the zip and pull it open. Reward him, once he can do this well. Repeat this exercise many times. You should work towards affirming your dog only when he manages to pull the zip open completely. Always bear in mind the size of your dog. You have to make sure that he is able to reach the zip.

If your dog has understood quickly what he is supposed to do, and he readily takes the zip without prompting, you can introduce a new command; for example 'Zip!' or 'Take off!', rather than keep using 'Pull!'

Even a smaller dog can open a jacket.

In order to take off the jacket the zip has to be opened completely.

Improvisation is everything: Even without sleeves, there are other ways to take off a jacket. (Photos: A. Maurer)

In order to take the jacket off completely, the dog only has to pull the sleeves. To achieve this, you withdraw your hand into the sleeve and take the end of the sleeve with your other hand. Have your dog pull the sleeve by giving the commands 'Take' and 'Pull!' Help him by slipping out of the sleeve and affirm your dog. Deal with the second sleeve in the same way.

Skateboarding

The dog climbs on a skateboard and rides it. Use a skateboard that is the right size for your dog. An older board with slow-moving bearings may be useful; perhaps you can find one in a charity shop or a car boot sale? On the first encounter between dog and skateboard, prevent the skateboard from rolling away by placing a small cushion underneath it, or by blocking the wheels with rocks. If you are used to working with a clicker, do use it for establishing first contact between dog and skateboard.

Then you can lure your dog onto the skateboard with a treat. Reward him as soon as his first paw touches the board. You can already use the command 'Skate!' at this stage. Once your dog climbs on the skateboard without any problems, you can gradually eliminate the braking implements. You should make sure the dog doesn't make his first attempts at riding a skateboard on a surface that is too smooth; a carpet on the other hand would be ideal. On a carpet, the skateboard won't roll as easily as on tarmac, and the dog can gradually get used

Thus secured, the skateboard cannot roll away.
(Photo: A. Maurer)

to the rolling motion. Since you are dealing with a new set of circumstances, go back to rewarding the slightest contact between a paw and the skateboard's surface. As soon as the dog puts both paws on the skateboard, it will start moving a little. Reinforce this by way of a treat. When this works well, try to increase the distance, little by little.

If your dog shows any signs of fear or insecurity on top of this wobbly vehicle, proceed only in the tiniest steps, or leave this trick out altogether.

Take a bow.

Scully is clearly enjoying the trip. (photo: T. Stens)

The simultaneous feeding with treats makes the first attempts easier.

After some practice, Benda balances the cup quite nonchalantly. (Photos: A. Maurer)

This trick requires a lot of confidence and practice in order to work. (Photo: A. Maurer)

Balancing objects on the rear

The dog stands in the bowing position while balancing objects that have been placed on his rear. As a requirement for this trick the dog ought to have already mastered the bowing position confidently.

You could have your dog balance a whole variety of objects on his behind. Start by using simple, flat objects. Often the dog will get up and have a look at the object as soon as you're about to place something on his rear. Allow the dog to have a good look at the object of your choice and give it a good sniff, so that he won't feel threatened by it. It may be helpful to feed your dog treats at the same time while placing the object on his rear.

Have your dog assume the bowing position while you touch the dog's posterior carefully with the object for the briefest of moments. Take the object off again straight away, and praise him enthusiastically. Develop this routine slowly: hold the object in place for one to two seconds before taking it off again. If the dog manages to balance the object for a few seconds, you can try to walk a couple of steps away from the dog.

If your dog co-operates well, you can develop this into a pretty spectacular trick. Have the dog balance a mug. A mug with a rather wide bottom would be helpful at the beginning, such as a special learn-how-to-drink-mug for children. Once this works well, you can advance another step by taking a bottle of water and pouring some water into the mug, while the dog balances it on his rear.

To begin with, pour in only a few drops, take the mug away afterwards and enthusiastically praise and reward the dog. Increase the amount of water little by little. As a reward, or for effect, you can also allow the dog to drink from the mug afterwards. If your dog keeps getting up the moment you start pouring, ask a second person to help by giving the dog a treat while you pour the first drops into the mug.

Here's Boomer

You may remember the children's television series 'Here's Boomer' from the 1980s. This cute fluffy dog used to prop up his paws against a climbing frame and poke his head between his paws. Any dog can do this, no matter what size

Gini is eagerly awaiting her treat.

A nose poked under the arm, and another treat is forthcoming. (Photos: A. Maurer)

it is. And you don't need a climbing frame either. Your dog can display the same exercise propped up against your arm. Take up a position so your lower arm is held between you and your dog. Hold your arm stretched out just above the height of your dog's head. Encourage him, by way of a treat, to stand up on his hind legs in order to reach it. Offer your arm for him to prop his front paws up against, and give him the treat while his paws are still on your arm. Keep him there for a while, and affirm this again and again with a treat.

This done, try to persuade your dog to put his head between his front paws with the aid of a treat. Take the treat and hold it below your arm between the dog's front paws. Reward even the smallest of attempts, as long as the dog still has both his paws on your arm.

Once your dog can do this exercise on your arm, you can start practising the same exercise on tree branches or fences during a walk.

Tidy up

Who wouldn't like to have a dog who does the tidying-up – even if it's just putting away his own toys. A clicker works best for developing this trick. Take a cardboard box or any type of box. The ideal size would be a box whose upper rim reaches approximately the height of the dog's chest. Put the box in the middle of the room and remove all toys except one. Hand this toy to your dog using the command 'Take!' Every movement with the toy towards the box should be rewarded with a click and a treat.

Jonny approaches the box with determination…

…and does some tidyingup. (Photos: A. Maurer)

dog with a particularly tasty treat. If your dog is good at fetching, you can have him take the toy and drop it into the box using the command 'Let go!' The only problem with this is that the dog will not necessarily associate the command 'Let go!' with putting the toy inside the box; or, in other words, that this exercise may take a while before he can do it at a distance.

Balancing treats and catching them

This is probably one of the most popular tricks, and will not fail to impress. The dog balances a treat on his nose; when a signal is given, he throws it up in the air, and then catches it in his mouth. For the last part it is important that the dog has already learnt catching treats with his mouth. Some dogs are naturally gifted for this; others may struggle a bit.

Try to aim the treat accurately while practising this with your dog. Have your dog sit and throw him a treat. Try to aim carefully. If your dog is good at catching things, every now and then throw the treat a little too far over to the left or a little too far over to the right. If he manages to catch these treats as well, he will probably be able to learn this trick quite quickly. If your dog doesn't catch the treat and it falls on the ground, don't let him eat it, but pick it up and throw it again. Don't practise with treats that are too tiny; the best to use are ready-made treats which are all the same shape and therefore easier for the dog to anticipate. Commercially available treats are also better placed

Because the dog has to drop the toy in order to get the treat, you can get him to drop the toy inside by skilfully placing the box in the right spot. At the same moment that the dog drops the toy, even before it hits the inside of the box, you give the command 'Tidy up!' Reward the

on the nose than, for example, chicken pieces. Choose a brand where the individual pieces are about the size of a thumbnail with at least one flat side, and stick to these for the time being. Every type of treat behaves differently while in the air, and during the learning phase a change of treat may be difficult for a dog to deal with. If your dog is very greedy, leave the treats out in the open for a few hours until they smell a little less attractive.

Have your dog sit, and lightly put your hand around your dog's jaws from below. Don't exert any pressure, tickle him a little with your fingertips, and reward him with a treat. The fact that you are holding on to his jaws should definitely not be misunderstood as a threat or a punishment by the dog. Hold him in this position and try to place a treat on his nose. He will probably try to raise his head in order to reach the treat.

To begin with, put the treat on the dog's nose for only a split second without letting go, and then give the dog a treat. As he will increasingly accept this, let go of the treat completely, praise him with enthusiasm and give him some really tasty treats. Slowly increase the time span during which the dog keeps the treat on his nose, until you manage a few seconds. Now let go of the dog's jaws, carefully and only very briefly. Make sure that the dog doesn't throw the treat up in the air, or let it slide off his nose straight away.

At the beginning, however, allow him to do so after just a brief moment by giving him an enthusiastic 'catch'. As before, keep increasing the duration. If your dog throws the treat up in the air but can't catch it, carry on practising by

Place the treat on his nose.

Let go only briefly at first, and reward him quickly.

This requires absolute self-control.
(Photos: A. Maurer)

Balancing the treat, and in control, despite the great distance.

Throwing the treat in the air also requires some practice.

The gaze firmly fixed on the treat.
(Photos: A. Maurer)

throwing treats from different angles. The dog has to learn to correctly judge the treat's trajectory, and then how to catch it.

At a later stage, in order to make the trick harder for your dog, you can walk around the dog or turn your back to him while he is balancing the treat.

Bear in mind that this trick requires extreme self-control on the part of the dog. Practise in really tiny steps, so you advance slowly, but steadily.

Opening drawers and cupboards

This is a lovely exercise from the world of support and assistance dogs for the disabled. The dog opens drawers and cupboards. In order to prevent the dog from getting it into his head to clear out all cupboards in the house, you can work with only one cupboard, and under very particular circumstances.

Take a short piece of rope, which you tie to the handle of the cupboard or the drawer. Make sure that the door doesn't slam shut again with a bang – or put a small piece of soft padding on the inside of the door. Your dog should never be startled while working. Lead the dog towards the rope that is attached to the cupboard while saying the commands 'Take' and 'Pull!' Reward him straight away, as soon as the door or drawer has moved by just a few millimetres. If the dog manages to open the door all the way, reward him with a jackpot. If the dog co-operates eagerly, and has quickly grasped that the

point of the exercise is opening doors and drawers, you can use a new command: 'Open!' In the initial phase you should always give the command at the point when the dog is about to start his action.

Of course, it is possible to do this exercise without the help of a piece of rope and to teach the dog to take hold of the door or drawer handle itself, pulling it open. For this there would need to be a knob which the dog can take hold of easily. Bear in mind, however, that this may enable your dog to gain access to cupboards which are not meant for him, and which may contain food or cleaning materials. This could be life-threatening for very nosy dogs and those who like to experiment. You can of course attach child safety catches to certain cupboards, and make them dog-safe this way, but you can avoid the problem altogether, by only teaching your dog to open doors which have a piece of rope attached to them.

At a more advanced stage, you can also have your dog fetch things from the cupboard after he has opened it.

Opening a pedal bin

The dog opens the bin by pushing down the pedal. You may want to think about whether you really want to teach your dog this exercise. Dogs love the precious leftovers that can be found in bins, and teaching them how to open them would come close to an open invitation. You can avoid this by practising with a small bathroom bin, which only contains toiletry waste, for

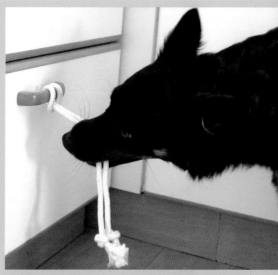

Once the principle has been understood, opening doors is easy.

The border collie mix Scully has to pull hard to get the drawer to open. (Photos: T. Stens)

instance. The foot pedal should be large enough for a dog's paw and the lid should easily open when light pressure is applied. Weigh down the bin by putting a rock or a bag of sand inside. When starting the exercise, wedge the bin between your feet, to prevent it sliding away.

The dog should have mastered the 'Touch!' command well beforehand. Point your finger towards the foot pedal and give the command 'Touch!' If the dog touches the pedal with his paw, reward him straight away. Affirm any contact with the pedal at first, even if the lid doesn't move perceptably. If the dog definitely touches the pedal, hold back the reward and wait until he pushes firmly enough to lift the lid slightly. Affirm your dog with a jackpot straight away. Work step by step towards the complete opening of the lid.

If your dog has already learnt how to tidy, you can gainfully combine the two activities by having your dog put away waste paper or similar things on his own.

A firm push is needed for the lid to open. (Photo: A. Maurer)

Head shake on command

Following a signal word, the dog shakes his head. This trick can easily be combined with a question-and-answer game. It is important that you never practise this with a dog who you don't know, or a dog whose previous history you are not familiar with. Because of the close proximity between your face and that of the dog, you have to know the dog really well and trust him and – what's even more important – the dog has to trust you and has to know that you are no threat to him.

Jonny shakes his head instantly when he feels the draught. (Photo: A. Maurer)

Sit down in front of your dog and blow against the upper inner rim of his ear. But please don't blow inside his ear! The draught should only tickle his ear slightly. Ideally this will make your dog shake his head. Reward this behaviour straight away. This is easier to practise with dogs whose ears are pricked up, than with floppy-eared dogs, because the draught doesn't reach the right spot if the ears are hanging down. In this case you can only practise this when the dog has his ears folded backwards.

While you are blowing, and the dog shakes his head as desired, you now have the problem that you can't blow and give a command at the same time, in order for the dog to make the correct association. It therefore would make sense to create a visual sign for this command first. A human head-shake can be quite an amusing visual signal for the dog, and to blow while shaking one's head isn't that difficult either. After repeating this a few times, just shake your head without blowing. If your dog also shakes his head, he has already understood, and you can carry on without blowing.

If your dog moves away to evade the draught, or shows signs of being unwell during this exercise, leave out this trick. Instead, you can practise a whole body shake. Have a treat ready when you take your dog swimming, and every time your dog emerges from the water and shakes himself to get rid of the excess water in his coat, you give him a command of your choice and then reward him for it. This works after a walk in the rain as well, and it is a real help when the dog shakes himself outside the front door, rather than inside the hall. This way

Once controlled by a signal the dog shakes his head as desired. (Photo: A. Maurer)

it may take a little longer to develop the command; it is important, however, that the dog doesn't feel uneasy or unwell in any way.

Walking backwards

There are two distinct ways for dogs to walk backwards: walking backwards in heel position together with the owner, and walking backwards away from the owner. The easier type is walking backwards together with you.

Take a treat, stand with your legs wide apart so that the dog fits in between. Make sure you are standing comfortably and then lure the dog to move between your legs from behind you, so you are both facing the same direction. Reward the dog as soon as he is standing between your legs. Take a treat, allow the dog to sniff it and 'pull' him with it in a backwards direction. You don't physically pull him in a literal sense, but you hold the treat above his head so that he has to take a step backwards in order to keep an eye on the treat. You reward this first step enthusiastically and give him the treat straight away.

Make sure the dog doesn't just sit down instead of taking a step backwards. Don't reward him in this case. A sitting dog cannot walk backwards. Try to hold the treat in a different manner: not above his head, but at the height of his breastbone below his nose. This way he has to take a step backwards again in order to keep the treat in his field of vision. If he does this, again reward the first step immediately. You proceed in exactly the same fashion if the dog

A treat can make this unusual movement palatable.

Standing a little more upright soon makes the exercise more fluid. (Photos: A. Maurer)

rises up on his hind legs in order to reach the treat.

Develop this very slowly, always adding just one more step. Once the treat-guided action works quite well, slowly stand up straight, and hold the treat in front of your chest.

Don't forget to reward all the small intermediate steps too, so you can eliminate all aids and accessories without any setbacks. As walking backwards with a dog between your legs is very difficult, and doesn't look particularly attractive either, you should aim to have your dog walk backwards by your side. If your dog usually walks on your left side, choose the right side for this exercise. This has the advantage that the dog knows instantly what comes next.

Only start this part of the exercise when the previous part has already been working well. A wall or a fence can be helpful for this. Position your dog between yourself and the fence and give the command for walking backwards. In an ideal situation the dog will actually take a step backwards. Reward him instantly. As a rule, however, the dog will miss having you stand above him. 'Remind' your dog, by proceeding in the same way as you did at the beginning of the exercise, only that this time the dog stands beside you. Make sure that the dog doesn't make evasive movements behind you, so you end up stepping on his paws when you walk backwards together. The fence makes learning to walk backwards in a straight line a little easier. Once this works well, try it without a fence.

One further variation is walking backwards around the owner. This involves the dog walking around you in a circle. Don't practise this

Walking backwards, in heeling position, has to be done in a straight line, otherwise there is a risk of falling over the dog. (Photo: A. Maurer)

straight after practising walking backwards, because it would confuse the dog unnecessarily, and make both tricks more difficult. With the help of a treat, you lead the dog backwards around you in a complete circle. If you find it difficult to pass the treat from one hand to the other behind your back, you can also turn around on the spot. As usual, to begin with, reward the first steps backwards. Once this works well, only give the reward after the dog has managed a complete circle around you.

The third option is that of walking away from you backwards. This is best achieved by training with the clicker or by very precise affirmation at the start of the exercise, best done with a conditioned word of praise. Once your dog is 'working' a few metres away from you, it is no longer possible to affirm him instantly with a treat. Affirm even the most hesitant move in a backward direction. You can prompt your dog to move backwards by moving towards him in a narrow passage way for example. The dog must never be made to feel threatened, however. One possible problem resulting from this is that the dog may start always moving backwards as soon as you move in his direction. It is therefore advisable to choose a route that will perhaps take longer, rather than having to invest a lot of time, later, in order to untrain an undesirable behaviour.

If your dog can walk a few paces backwards already, but makes a sideways detour, you can use broom sticks and stools to build an 'alleyway' for him, through which he can only move backwards in a straight line.

Moving away backwards is best developed using a clicker. (Photo: A. Maurer)

Regarding all three variations, you should establish the command for each exercise by using your chosen signal word during the first move in a backwards direction.

Crawling

The dog crawls forwards close to the ground. This is a very cute trick, which you should, however, only practise with a healthy fully grown dog. If your dog has arthritis or anything like that, please don't do this particular trick.

Have your dog assume the 'down' position. Take a tasty treat, allow the dog to sniff it, and hold it close to the ground just outside the reach of your dog's nose. If he edges forwards in order to reach the treat, reward him with it straight away.

He doesn't have to cover a great distance at the beginning, he should just learn that crawling forward leads to a quick reward. If the dog tries to get up, it may be that you are holding the treat too far away from him. It should be only just beyond his reach. You could create a learning aid by putting several chairs in a line, creating a low passage, and carry out the same

Hold the treat closely in front of the dog's nose. (Photo: A. Maurer)

exercise under those chairs where the dog cannot get up. If your dog is so small that he can walk comfortably under the chairs, you can build a similar construction out of cardboard boxes. As soon as your dog crawls in a forward direction, add the command 'Crawl!' Once this works well, practise the same thing without a treat in your hand. If the dog manages to crawl forwards following the command, praise and reward him enthusiastically.

Crawling backwards

This is practically the equivalent of the 'Royal' discipline. To teach a dog how to crawl backwards is very difficult, and only a few will ever learn it. Your dog should have mastered 'moving in a backwards direction' already. As before, the starting position is the 'down' position. You can use the chair tunnel positioned above the dog as a learning aid once more. Now give the command for walking backwards. The dog is prevented from getting up by the chairs, but will nevertheless try to carry out the backwards movement. If he moves backwards, even just a tiny bit, reward him instantly. Develop this backwards movement centimetre by centimetre. Once the dog has understood the point of this exercise and starts to crawl backwards, choose a new command for it, which must be very distinct from the signal word for walking backwards.

If you have a lot of experience with using a clicker, you could try to develop the behaviour freely without any aids and accessories. This requires you to have a very keen eye and a good knowledge of your own dog.

The right hand covers the right paw.

Crossing paws left over right

The dog is lying in the 'down' position and crosses his paws. Some dogs adopt this paw position naturally, in which case all you need to do is affirm this. If your dog doesn't display this behaviour normally, you can of course still teach it to him. He should, however, have mastered the handshake, left and right, beforehand. Kneel or sit in front of your dog. His paws are fully stretched out and point in your direction. Start with the dog's left paw.

Cover the dog's right paw with your right hand. Next put your left arm far over your right arm, with your palm pointing upwards and ask your dog to give you his left paw. Your arm should be sufficiently outstretched that the dog can basically do the handshake in the usual way. The only difference is the fact that this time

Dando is happy to hand over the desired paw. (Photos: A. Maurer)

Crossed paws give your dog an air of elegance. (Photo: A. Maurer)

your arms are crossed over. Reward the command once it has been carried out well.

Once the dog has got used to this peculiar position and does the handshake without any problems, take your left hand, on which your dog is supposed to place his left paw, a little further over to the left each time, centimetre by centimetre. Now the dog can no longer reach your hand by simply extending his paw, but has to put one paw across the other in order to fulfil the command. Once you have moved your hand far to one side, so that it is now positioned to the left of your right hand, slowly begin to 'sneak out' this hand. Keep covering your dog's right paw with your right hand for a little while longer, so he doesn't try offering it for a handshake in place of the left paw. Hold your left hand a few centimetres away from the side of your dog's right paw. Encourage him again to shake hands. Withdraw your hand just before the paw touches your hand. Now the left paw is lying across the right paw.

Praise your dog enthusiastically and reward him. Repeat this step until the dog puts one paw across the other without any problems, and reward him plentiful. Once this works reliably, add a new command for this exercise, for example 'Tap!' Now you just have to 'sneak out' the second 'helping hand'. Leave two fingers at first, then only one on top of the right paw and practise the whole thing in both positions about a dozen times. If the dog makes no attempt to use his right paw, leave out the second hand too. Now the dog has learnt how to cross the left paw over the right. If you want him to be able to do this the other way round as well, right

over left, you have to develop the exercise in the same way, only the 'wrong way round'. Depending on the dog, it may be easier to wait until he can do one side confidently and reliably in any situation, before you begin practising it the other way round.

Pushing a doll's pram

The dog pushes a doll's pram. This trick is really not that difficult to learn and offers many variations. You should be aware that the body posture required by this trick requires a great effort on the part of the dog, and is therefore not suited for a dog that is not fully grown or whose ability to move is impaired in any way.

You need a pretty sturdy doll's pram with a straight push bar whose height should preferably be adjustable. You may be able to find a suitable doll's pram cheaply at a car boot sale or from an online auction house. They are available in all sorts of sizes, so that this trick can be taught to smaller dogs as well.

Lean on the push bar yourself and apply a little bit of pressure in order to check how sturdy the pram is. If the pram tends to topple over easily, weigh it down by putting a big rock or two bags of bird sand inside. Next, you make sure the pram doesn't roll away. Allow the dog to sniff this new object thoroughly and reward any close contact with a treat even at this early stage. The dog should associate his first encounter with this strange new thing with a particularly pleasant experience. Put the dog in a straight position behind the push bar and hold

a treat above the bar just outside his reach. If the dog gets up on his hind legs in order to get to the treat and props up his paws on the bar,

The dog is lured into this position with the help of treats. (Photo: A. Maurer)

71

give him the treat straight away. If the dog remains in this upright position, feed him lots of treats, so that standing upright at the push bar becomes an especially desirable activity for him. Repeat this several times until the dog enjoys putting his paws on the bar and does so voluntarily.

Up to now the wheels were blocked; now the dog has to realise that the pram actually moves. Make sure that the surface under the pram's wheels is not too smooth – a carpet or a lawn would be ideal, as the pram should only move very slowly at the beginning. In addition you should safeguard against the pram rolling away suddenly by securing it with one hand. Once more, proceeding very carefully, lure the dog

A dog who has learnt to tidy up can also put dolls in prams. (Photos: A. Maurer)

Lure the dog with a treat to into a forward motion.

into an upright position with his front paws on the push bar. Make sure that the pram moves forward in an easy and controlled fashion, while giving the dog tasty treats at the same time. Should he feel uneasy, go back to the previous stage.

Once the dog and the pram are engaged in forward motion, give the command 'Push!' and reward the dog. Once this works well, try taking two or three steps at a time and reward the dog with tasty treats. Increase the distance slowly, but bear in mind that this position is very exhausting for your dog. Don't overdo practising this, but rather work in smaller, shorter sessions.

If you want to develop this trick further, there are several options to choose from. You could have the dog put a doll into the pram. This can be achieved without any problems if the dog has already mastered the 'Tidy up' command. If he cannot do this yet, teach it to him before practising with the doll and the pram.

In addition you can have the dog close the pram's hood. For this the dog should have already mastered the 'Closing the box' routine. Because dogs find it very hard to generalise, most dogs cannot apply the command to a new situation straight away. Start with a step-by-step approach once more. Encourage the dog to touch the hood with his nose. This works best while the dog is standing straight behind the

It works this way too. Take hood in mouth and pull upwards. (Photo: A. Maurer)

doll's pram, so that a slight forward and upward movement will close the hood. If the dog touches the hood, reward him instantly. If the dog nudges the hood hard enough to lift it up a little way, reward him with a jackpot.

It has to be said, this trick with all its variations is rather complex. Allow yourself and your dog a slow, thorough learning process. What has been described here briefly and in quick succession is not easy to learn. Don't lose your patience, and most importantly, don't lose your sense of fun.

Alternatively you can also have the dog push a small shopping trolley. Develop this trick works in the same way as before. You can also use other wheeled objects, like a large children's tractor, and other 'vehicles' are also possible. Just make sure there are no sharp edges, and the dog can't get caught on anything and hurt himself.

Baring of teeth

Lassie and all her doggie colleagues from the world of movies and TV – they can all do it: look menacing on command. For this you should be expert at using the clicker for your training, because it is extremely important to hit the precise moment for the affirmation.

Some dog trainers are teaching this by pushing up the dog's lips and then clicking and rewarding. After a short period, the dog would start to display this behaviour just before the trainer was about to push up his lips, and the dog could then be rewarded for it. This is certainly a possibility, but it might be very difficult to phase out this aid again afterwards.

You should never affirm the dog when he displays actual menacing behaviour for real. By doing this you would not just be praising the lifting of the lips, but affirming the dog's behaviour as a whole.

Try the following: take a large firm treat and wedge it between your thumb and your index finger. Hold it in front of the dog's nose so he can reach it easily. He will try to nibble it through your fingers, and most dogs tend to automatically draw their lips back slightly while doing so. This is the point, which you have to 'whittle out'. Click and give the dog the treat from between your fingers immediately. Then continue the exercise with a new treat. It can take a while until the dog manages to link the two actions with each other and then to be able to display the behaviour on command as well. The effort is well worth your while, however, and it is also

The hand position derived from holding the treat has become the visual signal for the 'Angry' command. (Photo: A. Maurer)

possible to very slowly increase the duration of this 'menacing' expression.

There are also dogs who will display this baring of teeth when they encounter unpleasant smells such as cigarette smoke, vinegar or cleaning agents. Please don't resort to using any of these to help things along. It is not very pleasant for the dog.

Sneezing

The dog sneezes at your command. This trick is a little difficult to learn. Before you do this trick you should either be able to use a clicker, or you have to praise your dog at a very precise moment, because this is a behaviour which you can only affirm when it is displayed accidentally. Try and think of situations in which your dog tends to sneeze. This can often happen when a dog comes out of the water after going for a swim. In this kind of situation you can have your clicker at the ready and affirm the dog's behaviour. At first your dog will probably not understand why he got the treat. Bear in mind that with this type of behaviour, which can only be affirmed sporadically and not very often, it will take a lot longer before the dog is able to display it on command. Nevertheless, you can practise it now and again, whenever you can. After all, this exercise doesn't require long practise sessions, but only a single action which you can reward. As before, please don't make your dog sneeze by exposing him to smells that are unpleasant for a dog.

Scratching

The dog scratches himself on command. For this trick you can use a command such as 'Fleas!' or 'Itch!' On the one hand you can shape the dog's behaviour freely when he occasionally scratches himself. Affirm him in his behaviour when he does so. If he offers this behaviour again straight away, and keeps scratching himself, give the chosen command and reward him.

If you don't want to wait until your dog offers the behaviour spontaneously, you can try the following. Many dogs join in with glee when you scratch them on the side of their neck all the way down to their shoulder. Give him the command and the reward at this point, and simply repeat the whole thing, if your dog is enjoying it.

Spelling

The dog spells his name or perhaps some other word. This trick of all tricks is probably the one that prompts the maximum astonishment in observers. You can use several different aids and accessories. The easiest way would be to collect large instant coffee tins and to stick or paint letters onto them. Next you thread a piece of ribbon or cord through the plastic lid so the dog has something to hold on to. After this follows the most important part: the preparation of the tins with various different smells. The simplest way of doing this is by using tea bags. Into each tin put a tea bag with a different flavour. Enough of the tea smell will penetrate through the hole you made earlier for the cord, allowing the dog to tell the different tins apart.

Begin with a short word, for example 'Hello'. For this you will need five tins, labelled with five different letters and filled with five differently flavoured blends of tea. Alternatively you can use spices, herbs or other strong-smelling substances. The dog should already have mastered the 'Bring' command. Begin with the tin that has the letter H on it, put it on the ground and encourage the dog to sniff it, to pick it up and to bring it to you. If this works without a problem, the tin has to be named. You could say: 'Fetch H!', but it would be better to say: 'Fetch the first (letter)!'

For future performances it will be even more impressive if, for example, you have stuck the individual letters of your dog's name on the tins. Then you can ask him to fetch the first letter of his name, followed by the second letter, and so on. In the eyes of the spectators you now have a dog who not only knows how to tell different letters apart, but one who can spell his name too. As your dog doesn't identify the correct tin by its label, but by its individual smell, you can have him spell all sorts of different words by simply changing the letters you stick on the tins.

Have the dog fetch the first letter many times, before adding a second tin into the equation. In order to see whether the dog associates the tin with the word 'First' already, put a ball or a different toy on the ground next to the tin and send the dog to fetch the 'first'. Once this works well, you can add the second letter.

Put only the tin named 'second' on the ground, and have the dog fetch it to you. If this works

Scully quickly goes for the correct letter and thus for the correct tin. (Photos: A. Maurer)

reliably after many repetitions, put another object next to it once more, perhaps the same ball you used to practise the 'first' letter, earlier. You really will need to repeat this many times, especially if you have never done any 'nose work' with your dog before. Once this works well in eighteen out of twenty attempts, it is time to put the 'first' and the 'second' together. Proceed slowly with this, and either have the dog fetch the one or the other letter for the time being. Don't change between letters and proceed in small steps. If this time the dog confidently gets it right eighteen times out of twenty as well, you can have him fetch the other one. Only when the dog seems completely confident, you can start adding a third letter.

Only add the next letter jar when the dog has no problem finding the correct letter, and is able to tell the different jars apart. A few months will have gone by, before you'll have worked out five different letters. But this spectacular trick is worth all the hard work in the end.

Going through the hoop is an easy exercise for Ronja.

Jumping through a hoop

The dog jumps through a hoop; this is the classic circus trick. Take an old hoola-hoop, or fashion a hoop, which you can adapt to your dog's size, out of a piece of garden hosepipe. Put the hoop on the ground, hold it upright and allow your dog to familiarise himself with it. Lure the dog through the hoop with the help of a treat. Reward him when he passes through the hoop without displaying any fear or shyness.

Even if the hoop is close to the ground, some dogs just enjoy jumping up high. (Photos: A. Maurer)

Should your dog be very timid, put the hoop on the ground at first, and make it literally irresistible for him. Begin by slowly bringing the hoop in an upright position and rewarding the dog for approaching it. If the dog walks through the hoop, give him a jackpot.

Once the dog has learnt to walk through the hoop, start holding the hoop slightly above the ground; lower for small, short legged dogs and higher for large dogs. As before, lure the dog through the hoop with a treat. If the dog has to jump in order to pass through the hoop, there is a good chance he may attempt to reach the treat by walking around the hoop. Quickly swivel the hoop round so it's facing the dog again, and lure him through it once more. You can hold the hoop a little lower again, until the dog jumps through it without problem. At the point

where the dog is about to jump, you say 'Jump!', in order to introduce this command.

Once your dog has learnt how to jump, you can begin to develop the variation of this trick that is really spectacular: the jump through a closed hoop. Take an old newspaper and cut or tear it into strips about ten centimetres wide. If you have a very sceptical dog, just attach a single strip to the top of the hoop and have him jump through it again, something you know he can do already. Once that works well, add another strip of newspaper and then another, until you have created a sort of a curtain made from newspaper strips for the dog to pass through.

For the next step cover the entire front of the hoop with whole newspaper pages. In order to make it easier for the dog to progress to the next skills level, cut long slits into the paper with a

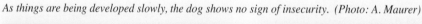

As things are being developed slowly, the dog shows no sign of insecurity. (Photo: A. Maurer)

dog show, and you may want to use something more attractive-looking, such as gift wrapping paper or silk paper instead of newspaper, bear in mind that this too will have to be practised beforehand. There are some dogs who perform this trick without a cut having been made in the paper beforehand. Personally I would always recommend preparing the hoop by making at least one cut. For the audience this is hardly – if at all – visible, and for the dog it makes this exercise a great deal easier.

A further variation of the jump through the hoop is the jump through your arms, linked up to form a circle. This can often be seen at Dog Dance events.

If the dog has already understood the 'Jump!' command, you can try to develop the jump through your arms without an assistant. Otherwise it is easier to have someone to help you, who can lure the dog through your arms and who can also affirm him instantly.

For small dogs, the jump through the arms is really easy, but it is also not impossible for medium-sized dogs. (Photo: A. Maurer)

carpet knife. Stick your hand and a treat through the slit, and demonstrate to the dog that it is actually possible to pass through the newspaper. Have him walk through slowly and make sure that the tearing of the paper doesn't scare him. Practise this many times before you advance to the next step, the jump through the paper. If you plan to use the whole thing for a

Stop the thief!

This is a familiar scene you might encounter on TV: The dog stops the fleeing thief by holding onto his trouser leg. It is important to wear an old pair of jeans whenever you practise this trick. Trousers made from linen or thin cotton can rip very easily if encountered with a dog's teeth, and even with jeans you might run a risk. The trousers should not be too tight, giving the dog something to hold on to. Don't ever perform this trick with assistants who don't know the dog, or who aren't aware what this trick

Most dogs like to play 'tug of war'. (Photo: A. Maurer)

involves, or who are very attached to their leg wear. Your intention and that of the dog could be completely misconstrued – at no point should anybody feel they are being attacked by your dog.

Take an old tea towel made from a durable material and have your dog pull it. If he already knows the 'Pull' command, you can make use of it. Pulling and playing 'tug of war' is self-rewarding. For this reason, make sure that the dog reacts to the 'Let go' command by immediately letting go of whatever it is. If he does this well, encourage him to engage in a new 'tug of war' game by making the towel flutter back and forth rapidly while giving the com-

mand 'Thief!' If your dog answers to this command every time and lets go when ordered to as well, go one step further and tie the tea towel around your ankle.

Tie the knot in such a way that one end is long enough for the dog to pull on it. It may be possible that some dogs will hesitate at this point, perhaps because they may have been taught as young dogs that pulling on a human being is wrong, or perhaps because they may have had a bad experience, and may have been kicked in the past. Once again, begin by taking small steps and motivate your dog with exuberance. If he takes the cloth in his mouth and pulls it, reward him instantly, even if it is done

Once the towel is firmly tied around the ankle, you need to stand firm. (Photo: A. Maurer)

a little hesitantly at first. When this works better and better, shorten the end of the cloth so the dog has to get closer and closer to your leg in order to pull the cloth. Make the cloth smaller and smaller and see if your dog will grab the trouser leg instead. If he does so, reward him straight away. Take off the tea towel and see whether the trick will work without it. If this is not the case, cut off a small piece of the cloth and attach it to your trouser leg with a few stitches. Don't use safety pins – the risk for your dog to injure himself would be too great.

Encourage your dog to pull, and reward him as soon as he does so.

Stop the thief! (Photo: T. Stens)

Jumping into your arms

For the next step, have the dog pull your assistant's trouser leg instead of yours. Stand directly next to your assistant, point to his or her trouser leg and give the command 'Thief!' If your dog goes full steam ahead for your trouser leg instead, don't hold it against him. He has not generalised this action yet and has to learn that the command applies to other trouser legs as well. This is why you have to affirm him even for the slightest attempt in the right direction.

But please, never abuse a command such as this in order to scare or startle someone. This would not be at all funny, and it could put your dog at risk and get you into serious trouble as well.

With a little run-up, the dog jumps into the arms of his owner. This trick should probably not be recommended unreservedly for every dog, or for every dog owner. If your dog is a St Bernard or a mastiff, you had better not try this trick. The same applies if you or your dog have a physical impairment. For the first attempts you should definitely wear long trousers and a long sleeve shirt, because the dog might inadvertently scratch you. A dog's claws can be very painful.

Begin by sitting on a stool or a chair, with the dog by your side. Encourage the dog to jump onto your lap. If your dog has already mastered the 'Up!' command, make use of it. Should your dog hesitate, lure him with a treat, and do some more work on the 'Up!' command, as described

The prospect of a treat makes any dog leap on your lap with joy. (Photo: A. Maurer)

Standing with slightly bent knees means that the dog has to overcome a greater height.

Ronja uses the thighs as a spring board for jumping into her owner's arms. (Photos: A. Maurer)

in the basic command section. If it works well and the dog jumps on your lap on command, pick a higher chair – a bar stool would be good – or sit on a table.

Have the dog jump in your arms again with the command 'Up!' Make sure that the dog really does jump from the side, because this way you can soften his jump with one arm, whilst at the same time using the other arm to support him from behind or under his tummy, depending on the dog's size. It is important to practise this while still sitting down, because for the next step you will actually have to catch the dog in exactly this way. For this you had better lean against a wall in a half-seated position while keeping your upper body straight. Only have the dog jump when you feel confident that you'll be able to catch him. If you or your dog are still not feeling too sure, practise the other steps for as long as it takes beforehand, until you are totally confident.

If you have a dog that is so small that jumping into the arms of an adult standing upright, would be too high for him, just kneel down. This position would be more suited to this kind of dog, and still provide a spectacular sight.

Balancing on a ball

The dog balances on a ball, almost ready for the circus. These days it is possible to purchase large gym balls in almost every sports store. They usually come in three different sizes and are not too expensive. These balls are excellent for the job. Choose a size to match your dog.

Benda feels reasonably happy on top of the ball. (Photo: T. Stens)

If your dog is very heavy or clumsy, or tends to lose his step easily, please don't do this trick. This exercise demands a great sense of balance, courage and confidence in you.

Pump the ball up quite hard, and allow your dog to sniff and to get to know this unusual object sufficiently. At the same time, roll the ball gently to and fro. Next you immobilise the ball. You can wedge it between your legs, or – and this would be particularly advisable for larger dogs – you can ask a second person to hold the ball firmly in a fixed position. You must not allow the ball to slide or roll away.

Don't let your dog jump straight onto the ball, even if he has already mastered the 'Up' command. The ball's particular shape, which pro-vides only a small curved area for the dog to stand on, requires a slow, sensitive approach. Persuade the dog to put his front legs on the ball with the aid of a treat. Do give him some more treats while he is in this upright position, propped up against the ball. Once your dog is not nervous of touching the ball at all, position yourself close to the ball. This works best if you also wedge the ball between your legs at the same time. Move your dog to your side and, with the command 'Up!', have him jump on the ball from there.

It is important that you soften your dog's jump well. Put one arm around his chest and the other around his hindquarters. Hold him securely, and first of all, allow him to find his bearings on top of the ball. When he has found his balance, keep holding him securely and reward him with a treat as well. Then have him jump off. It will take a very long time before your dog will be able to stand on the ball confidently and without your assistance. You must allow your dog this time, because finding and keeping his balance is a very difficult task to

perform for a dog. Small and agile dogs tend to find this trick much easier than larger dogs.

If your dog is very talented, after a few weeks you can begin to slightly move the ball from side to side. Make sure you do this on a soft and even surface, preferably a lawn, in order to reduce the risk of injury. The difficult part of walking on a ball is that the dog has got to walk backwards in order for the ball to roll in a forward direction. Don't under-estimate the level of difficulty of this trick, and proceed extremely slowly.

As a variation that might make things easier for some dogs, you could also use a roller instead of a ball for the dog to balance and walk on. For smaller dogs you could use a section of packaging tube from the inside of a rolled up carpet, for example; for larger dogs you could glue a piece of carpet around a food barrel. This version can be developed in the same way as with the ball, and just as slowly.

The ball must be held firmly in place, so it doesn't roll away when the dog jumps on top.

Sit up and beg

Simple and cute: the dog sits upright on his hind legs. From the 'sit' position you lure the dog with a treat into an upright position. At the beginning, do give him the treat as an affirmation, as soon as his front paws are lifted up in the air.

Accompany this with a command of your choice, for example 'Beg!' Develop this slowly until the dog is sitting in a securely balanced position on his hind legs. If your dog is fidgety and keeps trying to jump up to get the treat, use a slightly less attractive treat, or try to develop

This is how relaxed your dog should be, before you attempt to take the next step. (Photos: T. Stens)

himself. If your dog can do the 'Sit up and beg' with absolute confidence, try to combine this with the 'Act ashamed' command. This requires extremely good co-ordination, and a dog who is able to keep his balance with great confidence.

Poodle Mona can do a perfect 'Sit up and beg'.

Washing his face with his paws – almost like a raccoon. (Photos: A. Maurer)

this command by using your dog's normal dog biscuits.

A mega-cute variation is the 'Raccoon'. The dog simultaneously performs the 'Sit up and beg' and the 'Shame on you!' commands. This makes him look like a raccoon who is washing

Stand up and beg

Very similar to the 'Sit up and beg', as the dog's upper body is also in an upright position. The difference is that the dog doesn't sit on his hind legs, but stands upright. Take the treat and hold it above the dog's nose, just far enough away so he can't reach it. The treat should be attractive enough for him to want to stretch himself in order to reach it. As soon as he stands up on his hind legs, even if it is only for the briefest of moments, affirm him instantly and say your chosen command word, for example 'Stand!'

A nice, but difficult variation is walking on two legs, or dancing, which involves turning around on two legs. You can start practising this when your dog can confidently do the 'Stand up and beg'. Lure the dog into a forward motion by way of an attractive treat. This is quite a hard thing for a dog to do. If your dog has a propensity for back problems (which is very common in Dachshounds for instance), please avoid this trick altogether.

The Spanish step

The dog lifts his front paws up high while moving forward, and puts them down stretched out in front of him. This exercise actually originates from horse riding, but looks great when dogs do it too. At Dog Dance events it is especially popular with large slim breeds, but also with smaller dogs.

There are two different ways of teaching this to your dog. One possibility is to adapt this

The poodle Chalada can do a 'Stand up and beg' with assistance. (Photo: A. Maurer)

exercise from the handshake. For this, your dog should already be able to do the handshake with the left and right paw. If your dog is not yet able to differentiate between his left and his right paw, you will have to teach him this beforehand. This is quite simple: have your dog give you a handshake. Does he always use the same paw? Does he perhaps use the other paw, when you hold out your other hand to him? If this is the case, use a different command for the other paw. If the dog uses the wrong paw, there's no reward for him, but another opportunity to earn one. At the beginning don't yet alternate between paws, but practise consistently with one paw, and then with the other. Once this works well, have him do the handshake with one paw for a couple of times, and then give the command for the other paw. Does your dog use the correct paw without hesitation? If so, he must

have understood. If he is still unsure, keep practising and make it part of your daily routine. Handshakes can easily be practised for half a minute every now and then.

Have the dog stand and do handshakes while alternating between paws. Before his paw touches your hand, however, withdraw it quickly and give the chosen command, for example 'Olé!' or 'Ola!'. Make sure your dog keeps standing up and doesn't sit down during this. This way, you can save yourself the bother of having to teach your dog the same thing over again in a standing position. Once it works well while standing, you only have to manage the additional forward movement. In order to do this, take a treat, show it to your dog, and then close your hand tightly around it.

Hold it approximately at level with his nose, about one dog pace away in front of your dog,

An outstretched paw whilst moving forward earns a treat straight away.

and give him the command for the Spanish step. As soon as he lifts his first paw and has reached the highest point with it, you open your hand with the treat. He will move his paw downward, and also forward, in order to get to the treat. Practise this, taking turns between both paws.

It will take a while before you can start only rewarding every second step, then every third, and so forth. As soon as this works well for three to four steps in a row, you can bow down slightly less than before. Keep holding a treat in your hand at this stage, but when you affirm the dog, give him a treat out of your other hand. This ensures that the dog is not 'glued' to your hand, and you can gradually wean him off the hand altogether. Stand diagonally to your dog and practise from this position, because if you want to perform the Spanish Step side-by-side together with your dog one day, he has to learn to master the step without you walking backwards in front of him.

Alternatively you could develop this exercise with the help of a target stick. Your dog should already have learnt to touch the target stick with his paw for this. The advantage of the target stick is that you can start by standing upright next to your dog from the beginning. With a 'Touch!', in combination with the command for the respective paw, ask the dog to touch the target stick. Hold the target stick so the touch point is at about the dog's knee level, and a good half dog-pace in front of him. Reward the execution and follow on with the other side straight away. This will look stiff and gawky at first, and it will take a long time of practice, before these awkward movements are turned into fluid motion. However, this impressive trick is definitely worth the effort!

Taking turns between left and right produces a beautiful Spanish step. (Photos: A. Maurer)

Putting bottles in a crate

The dog puts empty bottles in a crate. This is a very useful trick, which can very easily be incorporated into everyday life. The dog should already have mastered the 'Tidy up' for this.

You need a crate and a few empty plastic drinks bottles that are the right fit. Choose the bottle size depending on your dog's size. In order to make it easier to sort the bottles into the crate, and to make them slide down bottomfirst, you can prepare them by making some alterations. Transparent candle gel from an arts and crafts shop is very suitable for this. With the candle gel you can add a bit of weight to the bottom of the bottle while it still appears to be empty. Pour the candle gel carefully into the bottle while it is still liquid, but let it cool down a bit first. Caution! Some bottles with particularly thin walls may not be suitable for this.

At first, familiarise your dog with just one bottle on its own. Have him pick up the bottle off the floor, or hand it into his mouth with the command 'Take!' Make sure he doesn't bite the bottle to pieces, though. The plastic shards could injure the inside of his mouth, or, if swallowed, lead to horrific perforations of the stomach. Encourage him to sort the bottles into the crate with a 'Tidy up', or whichever command you have chosen for tidying up.

Because dogs rarely generalise this sort of things very rapidly, it may be possible that your dog will now be completely in the dark as to what he should do next. If this is the case, develop this exercise afresh, exactly as you have done with the 'Tidy up' earlier, only this

Jonny purposefully approaches the crate…

…and puts the bottles inside.
(Photos: A. Maurer)

time instead of toys and box, use the bottles and crate. For a dog who has already mastered the 'Tidy up', this should only require a few practice sessions.

Polonaise

This is a fun trick, not just for party fans. The dog stands upright behind you and props himself up against your back or hip with his paws.

For this starting position the dog has to stand behind you, looking in the same direction as you. This is easily achieved by standing in front of your dog with a treat in your hand. Turn around quickly, so that you are now turning your back towards him while holding a treat behind your back at the same time.

The dog has his eyes on the treat instantly. Encourage him to try and get hold of the treat.

Hold it high enough to force him into an upright position in order to reach it. As soon as you feel a paw on your back, let him have the treat and praise him. If you have a large mirror at your disposal, practise in front of it; this makes it easier to determine when the right moment for giving the command has arrived, because you can see exactly when the dog is about to start the Polonaise.

As soon as your dog can do this well on command, increase the level of difficulty, and move forward slowly and carefully. Take only small steps to begin with, and keep an eye on how your dog reacts. If he puts all his paws on the

Standing behind each other like this is the correct starting position. (Photo: A. Maurer)

Reward the dog when he is standing upright nicely. (Photo: A. Maurer)

ground immediately, and walks not a single step upright behind you, you will have to employ the 'treat in the hand behind your back' once again. Have the dog nibble the treat from between your fingers, and take a careful step forward. If the dog walks a step with you, let him have the treat instantly and praise him.

Unfortunately this trick is impossible to do with very small dogs; even if you were to walk on your knees, your lower legs would be in the way.

Limping

At your command, the dog develops a limp, and is seemingly injured. This is probably the most difficult trick in this book. To get a dog to limp is very difficult and takes a long time. Start by teaching your dog how to stand on three legs. Decide which one of his two front paws should be lifted. Don't switch between paws, because this would make learning this trick unnecessarily difficult. If your dog offers standing on three legs by himself, affirm this behaviour and add a command, for example 'Paw!' If he doesn't offer this behaviour off his own back, try to touch his paw, massage and stroke it. Most dogs find this slightly disconcerting and lift up their paw as a result. You have to reward him the moment his paw is in mid-air. Make sure that the dog doesn't do a handshake, because if you affirm this, he won't understand what the trick is about. Only the paw in the air receives a reward. It would be best to work on this with a clicker, because at the beginning this moment can be very brief, and you don't want to miss it.

If your dog has learnt to lift his paw reliably at your command, gradually extend the period of time during which he has to hold his paw in this position. Starting with short sequences, you should increase the duration little by little. Reward him every time he stays in this position without putting his paw down until you tell him to. In order not to make this unnecessarily hard for him, increase the duration only by a second at a time.

If your dog manages to hold his paw up for about fifteen seconds, you can proceed to the next step. Let him nibble a treat from between your fingers while he is standing there with his paw lifted up. At the same time, move the treat very carefully and only by a few centimetres away from his nose, so that he has to move in order to keep nibbling the treat. Pay close attention to the paw in mid-air. The usual reaction would be to use this particular paw to take a step forward in order to get to the treat. Jog your dog's memory with the command 'Paw!', as soon as you become aware that his paw is moving downward slightly. To hit this exact point is very difficult and sometimes it will never work at all. If your dog becomes restless

Many dogs automatically lift a leg if you put a sock on their paw. (Photo: A. Maurer)

The leash as an aid is a good option, but it takes a long time to develop. (Photos: A. Maurer)

because of the treat, use a less pungent one and try again with that.

If the dog leans forward further and further in order to reach the treat, he will eventually limp forward with his paw still in mid-air. If you and your dog have managed this, have a party, praise and reward your dog enthusiastically, because he has achieved a tremendous success, and so have you. As soon as this is working well, continue practising and add a new command, for example 'Limp!' Once you have established the command, gradually increase the distance between you and your dog, but again, proceed extremely slowly.

It is quite possible that although you practise and practise, the trick steadfastly refuses to work. Don't get too frustrated, and don't carry on practising with clenched teeth. Never forget that this is something you and your dog are both supposed to enjoy.

You can, however, try a different method. Take an old baby's sock, or use one of those paw protectors, should you have one, and put it on your dog's paw. Many dogs don't like the feeling, and won't use the paw with the shoe or the sock on it at all. You can then affirm this behaviour and add a command. Eliminating the sock afterwards can be a little tricky, and may take some time. The sock can be 'shrunk' bit by bit by cutting little pieces off it until it is completely gone.

Another possible accessory to help this trick along is a leash or a rope. If your dog has mastered the 'Paw!' command and manages to stand on three legs for a period of time, take both ends of a good length of rope so you end up with an open loop. Don't tie the ends together. Otherwise your dog could hurt himself seriously, if he were to jump sideways suddenly. Just hold the ends very loosely, so you can quickly let go of the rope in an emergency. Give the dog the command for lifting his paw. Slip the loop over his paw so that it rests inside like an injured arm in a sling. Take the treat and let the dog nibble it through your fingers again. Move it away from his nose by only a tiny distance at a time, in order to encourage him into a forward motion. Once in the 'sling', the dog can't put his paw on the ground any more; by using the sling, you prevent him from doing so. As a result the dog limps forward. Affirm and praise him instantly. If the dog limps after the treat, add the command 'Limp!' After a while you will notice that the dog is putting less and less weight on the sling, and is beginning to limp more independently. Weaning the dog off this aid can take a long time, but don't be discouraged.

Skipping with a rope

The dog skips with a rope in tandem with you. Of course, you will have to be able to skip with a rope yourself for this. If it's been quite a while, you should get some practice without the dog first.

This trick is best suited for small to medium-sized healthy dogs who like to jump. First of all the dog has to learn how to jump up in the air. For this purpose take a ball, or one of your dog's other highly desirable toys. Hold it high above him, so he has to jump up in order to reach it. If he shows no inclination to jump, play exuberantly with the toy and the dog. Following on from this dynamic play, carry out the same exercise once more. If he jumps up after it, praise him and give him the toy straight away. Repeat this exercise and give the command 'Jump!' every time the dog is about to jump. Be careful not to work your dog too hard. You should practise tricks such as this one, which require intensive movement, only for short periods at a time, but you can do this several times a day. When your dog jumps up in the air confidently at the command 'Jump!', start jumping up simultaneously with your dog. Bear in mind that the rope will have to swing around both of you, so you have to skip very closely together. Don't forget to reward your dog for a competent execution. Again, don't practise skipping too many times in a row, but rather incorporate it into your daily routine, whenever you can spare a moment. It can be great fun skipping together with your dog for two or three skips; in the kitchen, at the bus stop, in the park.

Start by familiarising your dog with the rope. He should be moving in a relaxed manner, even when the rope is moving fast. Start moving the rope around the dog in slow, wide arcs. If he is relaxed doing this, reward him in between, and swing the rope in increasingly tighter and faster arcs. Your dog should not display any fear or insecurity at any point. If this is the case, however, you will have to proceed even more slowly and with extreme care. If the rope doesn't scare him from a distance of two metres onward, begin two and a half metres in front of him. Gradually desensitise him by approaching only a few centimetres at a time. Feed him with

For a dog of this size, skipping with a rope requires immense co-ordination and poise.
(Photos: T. Stens)

the rope lying next to him. If your dog shows any signs of distress, skip with your dog without a rope or choose a different variation, such as skipping with an elastic band. Many dogs have had a bad experience in the past. Humans who swing objects, or in this case, rope, can seem very threatening. There is no trick for which it would be worth risking your dog's trust in you.

Once your dog is completely relaxed dealing with the rope, you can start your first attempt at skipping with it. If you can get two helpers to swing the rope for you, it would make things easier at the beginning, because you'd only have to concentrate on jumping up in the air together with your dog at first. If you haven't got any helpers available to you, don't despair. Just concentrate on the first skip, and don't attempt to do several skips in a row. Only when you no longer have any problems skipping and swinging the rope at the same time, should you try to do more than one skip at a time.

But don't overdo the skipping either, because it is very exhausting for your dog.

Slipping on the leash

The dog picks up the leash off the ground, brings it to you and then sticks his head through the collar section. You will need a retriever or agility leash for this trick, because these have collars that can simply be slipped over the head. With this type of leash you don't have to worry about closing the collar with a buckle, as you would a normal leash.

Hold the collar section wide-open, like a lasso, in front of the dog's head and encourage him with a treat to stick his head through the loop. Affirm him as soon as he sticks is nose through it. Gradually lure him further and further through the loop.

As soon as he pushes his nose through the neck loop, say your command, for example 'Head!' This is quite easy to learn, and dogs like this trick, because for most dogs the leash represents a promise of fun and going for a walk.

If your dog has understood what this trick involves, put the leash on the ground in front

of you, and encourage him to pick it up. Use the command 'Take!', if your dog has already mastered this. Later, you can have the dog bring the leash to you, and then you only need to hold open the neck loop for the dog to slip his head through.

This dog sticks his neck through the loop in order to reach the treat. (Photo: A. Maurer)

The first contact can also be with a paw.

Jonny has grasped the issue and lightly nudges the lid upwards with his nose.

Opening a box

The dog opens a box on his own. For this trick you will need a box that matches the size of your dog. It should be stable and sturdy, and have a lightweight lid. There are many different types of inexpensive boxes on offer in furniture stores. The main thing is that the box doesn't slide away at the first practice attempt, thus making opening it unnecessarily difficult.

Place a large rock, or two bags of bird sand inside the box. In order to make it easier for your dog, you could attach a strap with a loop to the lid. Make sure that the lid in particular has no sharp edges. If you use a wooden box, it has to be very smooth, so the dog won't risk getting a splinter.

Lead the dog to the box slowly and allow him to sniff the box. Affirm him with the clicker or a treat, as soon as his nose touches the lid of the

A firm nudge opens the lid completely.
(Photos: A. Maurer)

the box. This alone can provide sufficient incentive for many dogs to want to find a way to get into the box.

If you have a very small dog, or you can't find a box with an opening lid, you could convert an old shoe box into a suitable box by using scissors and a bit of sticky tape. Cut a slit in the middle of the lid and pull a piece of a strap through it, tie the two ends into a knot, and you have a lid with a loop to hold on to. Affirm the dog when he touches the strap. If he knows the command 'Take', use it in order to get him to take hold of the strap and to lift the lid with it. Make sure that this type of box is also sufficiently weighed down by putting something heavy inside.

Closing a box

After your dog has learnt how to open a box, naturally the next step is to close it. The level of difficulty depends on the type of box. If you have picked a box with a foldable lid, this is perhaps easier, because the lid automatically comes to rest in the right position. Encourage your dog to nudge with his nose against the bottom section of the folded-back lid. Affirm every attempt, until the lid has been lifted up by a noticeable amount. With a good push, the lid is given enough momentum to make it swing back into the closed position. If the dog manages to do this at his first attempt, a jackpot is in order.

If you have decided to go for the shoe box option, you should adapt a slightly larger

box. Encourage him to take hold of the strap or to nudge the lid with his nose.

Affirm your dog instantly as soon as the lid lifts up, even if it's only a few millimetres. Once the dog has understood that the point of this exercise is to lift the lid, increase the level of difficulty and only affirm when the lid lifts up by a noticeable amount. Carry on doing this until the box is actually fully opened. In order to motivate the dog even more, you can let him watch you while you tidy his favourite toy into

Closing a folding lid is easily done.
(Photo: A. Maurer)

Switching on the light

The dog works the light switch using his nose or his paw, and switches the light on. Depending on the dog's size and the height at which the light switch is positioned on the wall, you may need a stepladder. If you are worried about your wallpaper, buy a small tablemat at a household supply shop and cut into it an opening a little smaller than the size of the switch face. First switch off your electricity at the mains. Take off the light switch, put the table mat over the wallpaper, and remount the switch again afterwards, and there you have your protective wallpaper cover.

Point to the light switch while using the command 'Nudge!', and encourage the dog to touch it with his nose. If you have worked out this command by using a sticky dot and you have not phased it out yet, then stick a dot on the switch. Position it slightly off centre, but on the exact spot where you actually have to apply the pressure in order to switch the light on. Affirm any contact at first. As soon as the dog firmly associates this with the switch, wait until the dog pushes hard enough to actually switch the light on. Reward this action generously – a jackpot would be best – and let him carry on trying out the switch. When you are sure that he has understood what he is supposed to do, add the command 'Light!'

If your dog drools a lot, I would suggest you go for the paw option for switching on the light, as opposed to having him use his nose. This works very much the same way. Use the command 'Touch!' for this. Bear in

second lid from a larger shoe box that fits loosely on top of the smaller shoe box. It is not that easy even for a small child to close a cardboard box properly, but for a dog it is a very difficult task indeed.

The art is to hit the exact spot on which to apply the pressure.

For long claws, a protective cover around the switch can be a good idea. (Photos: T. Stens)

mind that it might be not just the wallpaper that will suffer, but also the switch itself, if the dog scratches at it a lot at the beginning.

If you don't want your dog to jump up against the wall, use a small stepladder or a stool, and teach the dog how to jump up on one of those beforehand. If your dog still doesn't manage to reach the light switch, even with the help of a stool, you don't have to do without this trick. Get a push light from a household supply shop. These are battery-operated lights that can be switched on by simply pushing the light itself. They can be placed on the floor or mounted on the wall at the required height. You should not use ordinary table lamps, for safety reasons. Their switches

are often very small and not insulated properly, so that your dog's saliva might get inside and, in the worst-case scenario, cause an electric shock.

Stealing money

The completed trick should involve your dog walking up to a rucksack, opening the zip in the front pocket, taking out a purse, opening it and pulling out the notes inside.

This is probably one of the most sophisticated tricks around. As it requires a complex chain of action, the trick is subdivided into its separate components. First of all you need all the aids and accessories for this trick: an old purse that opens easily; a bank note – although at the beginning you had better use a piece of paper cut to size; a rucksack or bag with a front pocket offering enough room to accommodate the purse; a heavy rock, as well as some newspaper. You need the rock to weigh down the rucksack in order to prevent the dog from dragging the whole rucksack along with him, while attempting to open the zip. The newspaper is crunched up and used as stuffing for the rucksack in order to make it more substantial. Take a look at the zip: does it only have a metal zipper, or does it have a small ribbon attached to it? Dogs tend to dislike having to grip pure metal zippers. Make your dog's job easier by tying a small ribbon to the zipper that is less difficult to take hold of.

Looking at the way this trick is structured, the final action consists of pulling the bank note from the purse. This is where you begin. Show your dog the open purse with a large section of the bank note sticking out.

Encourage your dog to grip the bank note and to pull it out, using the command 'Take!' Affirm every gripping or pulling action. Once this works quite well while you are holding the purse in your hand, next put the purse on the ground with a large section of the note sticking

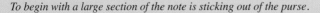

To begin with a large section of the note is sticking out of the purse.

out again. If the dog has grasped the principle of what is asked of him, he will quickly pull out the note once more. Make sure that the dog isn't standing on the purse while doing that, as bank notes are not particularly strong and will tear quite easily in combination with dog saliva. In order to make it more difficult, start pushing the note further and further inside the purse, thereby gradually reducing the section sticking out. Just to make it a little easier for your dog, a small corner may be left peeking out, even at the final stages. After a bit of practice, the dog will be able to pull out the note.

Now you close the purse. If the design is simple, and it just folds open, you can leave it

to your dog to work out the solution. Since he knows already that a treat is coming his way as soon as he pulls out the note, he will unfold the purse with his nose quite quickly. If the purse has a push button, don't close it completely at first, or wedge a small piece of paper inside the push mechanism so it's easier to open.

To help things along you can also put a treat inside the purse's centre fold in order to give your dog more of an incentive to open it.

Always have the dog carry out the trick until completion. This means that you don't just practise opening the purse on its own, but you have the dog pull out the note from inside the

Benda uses her teeth in order to open the purse. (Photos: A. Maurer)

Pulling out the purse is something most dogs will learn quickly.

Opening the zip is the final unit and the beginning of this trick. (Photos: A. Maurer)

purse after he has opened it as well. By doing this you will firm up the chain of action. The dog knows exactly what to expect next, and this way he will learn to link the individual actions together.

Once both individual actions have been securely linked with each other you can advance to the next stage: taking the purse out of the rucksack. Leave the pocket containing the purse wide open. Put the purse inside it, but make sure that about two-thirds of the purse is sticking out at the top, so the dog can take hold of it easily. Encourage the dog to take the purse out of the pocket by using the command 'Take!' If he is a bit slow at first, affirm the intermediate steps as well, and give him a treat for pulling the purse out of the pocket. If he is having hardly any problems at all with that, have him run through the whole procedure right to the finish and affirm him with a jackpot. Next, stuff the purse deeper into the pocket, deep enough to make it possible to close the zip. If the dog manages to extract the purse without any problems, this would be a remarkable achievement and you can proceed to the next stage.

Close the zip of the pocket containing the purse. Encourage your dog to take the zipper into his mouth and to pull on it, using the commands 'Take' and 'Pull!' Make sure the ruck- sack is weighed down sufficiently to prevent it being dragged across the room as the dog pulls on the zipper. At the beginning, reward him if the zip moves by just a tiny amount. If the dog manages to pull it open all the way, reward him with a jackpot. Join up the complete chain of action, and you end up with a fantastic trick, which will impress even the most experienced dog aficionados.

Conclusion

My dog can't do this!

Please don't underestimate your dog. Start with small things that give your dog a realistic chance of getting a treat and the feeling of having done well. If you are enthusiastic about it, your dog will take his cue from you. Approach your goals step by step, and don't try to do too much at once. Maybe your dog needs to do it another way. The methods described here are of course not the only ones that have any validity. Just as with 'normal' dog training, there are many ways that can lead to success. Not every method or every way is suitable for every dog. If you have taught your dog a trick another way, or if you have a different approach accessible to your dog, then that would be marvellous. Find the right way for yourself and for your dog.

Final refinements

Dogs are really bad at generalising. If you always practise under the same conditions, at the same time of day, and in the same location, your dog will find it very difficult to perform a trick he already knows to the same standard when the circumstances are different. At the beginning, practise in many different but undisturbed and quiet locations. Next, you could attempt a 'Shame on you' or a 'Play Bow' in a busy street, or you could try the whole thing while your family is sitting down for dinner. If your dog has no problems whatsoever with this, you can advance to the next step.

And what do I do with all these great tricks?

Once your dog has mastered a few of the tricks, you would probably like to show them off to somebody. Find yourself a grateful audience for your first 'performance'. Children tend to make very enthusiastic spectators, and very tolerant ones at that, just in case the trick doesn't work out the first time round.

If you have been gripped by 'trick fever', and your dog has also developed a liking for showing off the odd trick in public, you could always offer to make a contribution to your local animal shelter summer festival. Also, every now and again TV and film castings are held, where you can compete with other dog owners and their dogs. They can provide an amusing diversion and could be really fun. In addition there are always many new ideas to pick up, and you can learn a lot from the other participants.

Please always bear in mind your dog's well-being. If he is out of his depth in situations like these, your decision should always be based on what's best for him. Tricks are meant to be fun, and everyone involved should be able to enjoy. If your dog has mastered the tricks, but feels uneasy performing them in front of an audience, use your creative powers: Write down all the tricks your dog can do, and think about how you can package them into a little story. Put together a script and film the whole thing with a video camera. There are no limits to your imagination.

Too much nonsense?

Some people may ask themselves, why on earth should anyone want to teach 'something like that' to a dog? Well, no dog – apart from very few Hollywood exceptions – has to be able to balance on a ball, steal money or stop a thief. In this instance, it is true to say that the journey itself is in fact the reward. It does not matter at all how nonsensical the trick may seem in the eyes of some people; this is about the owner spending quality time with his canine partner, his best friend. The owner gives the trick some thought, learns how to break up the task into small steps, and works out how best to construct a chain of action. And because the whole thing is 'of no consequence', the owner not only approaches the

On the command 'Take', the dog can even learn how to hold a baby's dummy. (Photo: A. Maurer)

matter in a completely relaxed manner, but usually with a great sense of fun as well.

The dog basically doesn't mind what the task involves; to him, the main thing is that the reward, the environment and the atmosphere are good. That's why dogs are so keen to learn tricks. Often their owners are much more relaxed and laid-back when dealing with seemingly unimportant things. The relationship between the two can clearly benefit immensely from this atmosphere of relaxed learning. The laid-back mood and the experience of actually working together successfully will often transfer to the learning of other things as well, for instance in the area of obedience training. Make the best of this positive development.

And don't worry: even though my dogs know how to work light switches, I have never yet woken up at night to find all the lights in the house had been switched on. Nor do my dogs pick up rubbish in the park unprompted and put it in the rubbish bins. They know exactly how to calculate the probability of getting a reward, and they act accordingly. This is why, once you control a behaviour via a signal, you should no longer reward it, when the dog displays it without being prompted. Otherwise, you may one day have to face the rather embarrassing prospect of having to explain to your neighbour why your dog is attached to his trouser leg.

Thanks

Above all, I thank my dogs from whom I feel privileged to have learned so much, who are always there for me and who make my life so much richer. Without Benda, who has made such a lasting impact on my life, this book would never have been written.

I also thank my parents, who always backed me up in all the challenges I have confronted in my life; my daughter Jana, who found the idea of writing a book incredibly exciting; my friend Bianca Gricer, who has been so pleased for me and who was the first to get to read some sections of this book; my favourite Andrea (Gerhards), who has nothing whatsoever to do with dogs, but who will nevertheless read this book - won't you, Andrea? And Nicola Karpinski who, despite her young age, is so intuitive with dogs, and about whom I'm sure we will hear much more in the future.

I also thank Jessica Kornrumpf and Björn Tigges who discovered Scully, and who convinced me that I wanted to own a border collie mix after all.

Thanks to the photographic models:
Björn and Jessy lent me the support of as many as three dogs: Ronja with her dreadlocks; Emma, the border collie with a special charm; and Dando who was able to enchant everyone by just casting them a look, who tragically died just a few weeks after this book was first published. Dando, thank you for so many great pictures. You are deeply in our hearts. Thanks to Jonny, Nicola's dog who has contributed so

much to so many pictures with his unbelievable skills; Melanie Picciallo and Luke, the ultimate power dog; Meike Berghaus with Princess Gini.

Mandy Kositza with Laika, the dog with the prettiest ears in the world; Heike Wolf with Mona and Chalada, who invokes in you a great enthusiasm for this marvellous poodle breed; Sabine Maurer with Matjes for spontaneously jumping in the breach; and thanks to Hildegard Stens and Ex-Lab-Beagle Snoopy.

Thanks to Chrissi Steck for being so spontaneous, for re-reading the English version and adding helpful tips.

A special thanks to our photographer Andreas Maurer, who has put everything in the right light, with a keen eye and beautiful ideas. And I also thank Boomer, who is possibly the most important 'person': the children's series 'Here's Boomer', broadcast in the 1980s, has really shaped me, and made me cry during almost every episode. I always wanted to have a wonderful friend like that, who can do so many things. Lucky me: I've got two of them!

Have I forgotten anybody? But of course! Last, but not least: I want to thank you, the readers of this book with all my heart. It's wonderful that you are giving some thought to spending quality time with your dog. I hope that you'll have a lot of fun applying and working on new ideas. If I have learned one thing, it is the fact that these tricks are addictive, and you will be constantly on the look-out for new ideas. With this in mind, I hope that I was able to inspire you, and I finally wish you a fantastic time with your four-legged friend.

For further information, check out my website www.trickdogging.com.